did you know...

First published June 2009 by Dún Laoghaire Rathdown County Council,
County Hall, Dún Laoghaire, Ireland.

Permission to use or reprint any of this publication must be obtained directly
from Dún Laoghaire-Rathdown County Council.

ISBN 978-0-9557829-2-3

Cover: photograph of Pater and Ned, a bronze sculpture by Rowan Gillespie, Sandyford Village.

INTRODUCTION

This publication celebrates the unusual, the overlooked, the taken for granted and the forgotten aspects of this county's heritage. It features items that we may walk past every day or may be tucked away and out of sight. It is a reminder that our heritage does not always consist of the famous and the obvious. This publication is the outcome of two exhibitions that were produced in 2007 and 2008. These exhibitions were the result of a close collaboration between the Heritage Office of Dun Laoghaire-Rathdown County Council and the South Dublin Association of An Taisce (Veronica Rowe, David Rowe, Sue Pedlow, Ken Mawhinney, Norman Campion and Maura Mhic Giobuin).

We would like to thank the following people for their assistance with a number of photographs and information for this exhibition - Catherine Malone, Dr. Ron Cox of TCD, Ian Elliot, Tom Blake of the Dublin Institute for Advanced, Studies and Dr. Charles Mollan, Tony Kinsella, the staff of Concept2Print, Edmund Morris, Mount Anville School, Jill Sidall, Guinness Diageo Archives (especially Deirdre Flood), Brian Crowley of Kilmainham Gaol Museum, Niall Hatch and Michael Ryan of Birdwatch Ireland, Joss Lynham, Ray Bateson, Professor Stephen Zyliak, Dalkey Castle and Heritage Centre and Deirdre Ní Mhurchu. There are two books that deserve special mention for informing a number of sections of this book. They are 'Between the Mountains and the Sea' by Peter Pearson (O'Brien Press 2007) and 'The Antiquities of Old Rathdown' by Chris Corlett (Wordwell 1999).

It is the ongoing policy of Dún Laoghaire-Rathdown County Council to encourage the appreciation and enjoyment of the County's heritage. Each of the geographic sections of this book has an indicative map showing the general locations of the topics. We hope that this will encourage you to not only read about the heritage of the county but also to go out and see it for yourself.

Tim Carey
Heritage Officer
Dún Laoghaire-Rathdown County Council
June 2009

CONTENTS

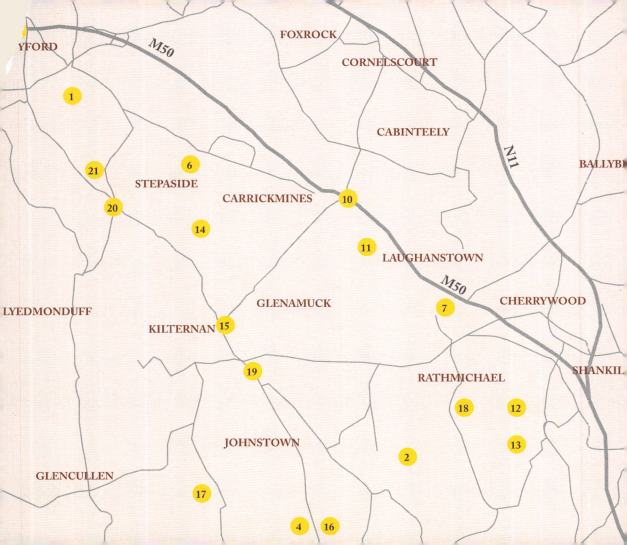

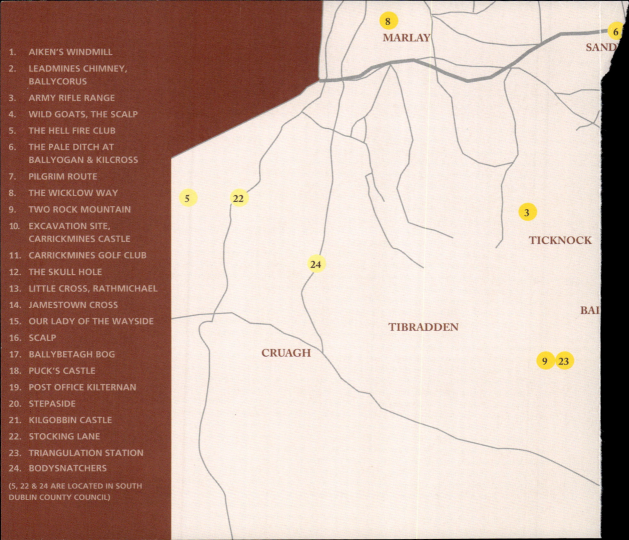

1. AIKEN'S WINDMILL
2. LEADMINES CHIMNEY, BALLYCORUS
3. ARMY RIFLE RANGE
4. WILD GOATS, THE SCALP
5. THE HELL FIRE CLUB
6. THE PALE DITCH AT BALLYOGAN & KILCROSS
7. PILGRIM ROUTE
8. THE WICKLOW WAY
9. TWO ROCK MOUNTAIN
10. EXCAVATION SITE, CARRICKMINES CASTLE
11. CARRICKMINES GOLF CLUB
12. THE SKULL HOLE
13. LITTLE CROSS, RATHMICHAEL
14. JAMESTOWN CROSS
15. OUR LADY OF THE WAYSIDE
16. SCALP
17. BALLYBETAGH BOG
18. PUCK'S CASTLE
19. POST OFFICE KILTERNAN
20. STEPASIDE
21. KILGOBBIN CASTLE
22. STOCKING LANE
23. TRIANGULATION STATION
24. BODYSNATCHERS

(5, 22 & 24 ARE LOCATED IN SOUTH DUBLIN COUNTY COUNCIL)

MARLAY

SAND

TICKNOCK

BAI

TIBRADDEN

CRUAGH

did you know...

Lána Stoicín
STOCKING LANE

?

THE MOUNTAINS

The purpose of the windmill was to supply electricity to Frank Aiken's house. However, it was not long in use when the sails blew off. Its frame has stood alone for many years.

This frame is made of four mighty poles that rise up like a pyramid. They stand on wheels which in their turn are supported on a circular concrete track, thus allowing the whole frame to rotate to achieve maximum benefit from the wind. Although it is now a relic it was once cutting-edge technology.

...THAT THE STRUCTURE KNOWN AS AIKEN'S WINDMILL IN THE FIELD BEHIND AIKEN'S VILLAGE IN SANDYFORD WOULD HAVE PLEASED ENVIRONMENTALISTS WHEN IT WAS CONSTRUCTED

?

LEADMINES CHIMNEY BALLYCORUS

The complete chimney or flue is over one kilometre long. It snakes its way up from the old lead works in the valley below to the landmark chimney on the hilltop. The stone tunnels are high enough for a person to walk inside.

In the days when lead was worked below, the fumes rose up the hilltop through this flue. These fumes contained minute lead particles and arsenic which were both poisonous substances.

Periodically, work was stopped to allow the flue to cool. The doors to the flue were opened to allow barrowfuls of lead deposits to be scraped out. Many workers died of lead poisoning giving the surrounding area the nickname "Death Valley".

...THAT THE LANDMARK LEADMINES CHIMNEY AT BALLYCORUS IS JUST THE TIP OF THE ICEBERG, SO TO SPEAK

?

ARMY RIFLE RANGE

Walkers on the mountain were alerted that the range was in use by a red flag flying near the forestry path.

The targets were operated by 12 men in a concrete dug-out who used levers to raise and lower them safely. Bullets smashed into the hillside, and 30 years later they are still plentiful for those who wish to look for them.

...THAT THE DISUSED ARMY RIFLE RANGE ON THE SLOPES OF THE THREE ROCK MOUNTAIN AT TICKNOCK WAS IN USE AS RECENTLY AS THE 1970's

?

WILD GOATS
THE SCALP

You can enjoy this Mediterranean experience by going no further than The Scalp and viewing these fine goats in natural surroundings. These goats are fairly recent arrivals, taking the place of many generations of feral goats. The Scalp is also home to deer and badgers.

Dubliners in the past would journey out – by bicycle, car and pony and trap – to enjoy the sights and refresh themselves at Butler's Tea House (now a private residence).

...THAT THIS IS NOT A SCENE IN CORSICA OR SARDINIA

?

Damaged by a storm, the roof was rebuilt with massive masonry which is still in place today. The lodge was sold to Richard Parsons, 1st Earl of Rosse, a member of the Hell Fire Club, which then transferred some of its activities to the hunting lodge.

The building was damaged by fire in the 1750s, and has not been much occupied since then. The Hell Fire Club was founded by the "bucks and bloods" of Dublin, 18th century young men of fashion who were notorious for their drinking and wild conduct. As horsemen, they may well have used the mounting block (shown here).

The history of the Hell Fire Club has many lurid and interesting stories associated with it, including the apparent appearance of the Devil one stormy evening.

...THAT THE BUILDING KNOWN AS THE HELL FIRE CLUB ON MOUNTPELIER HILL, RATHFARNHAM, WAS BUILT AS A HUNTING LODGE IN THE EARLY 18TH CENTURY

?

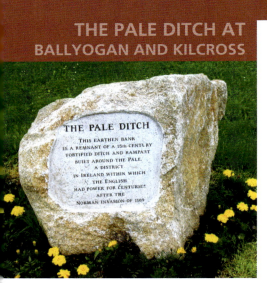

THE PALE DITCH

THIS EARTHEN BANK
IS A REMNANT OF A 15th CENTURY
FORTIFIED DITCH AND RAMPART
BUILT AROUND THE PALE.
A DISTRICT
IN IRELAND WITHIN WHICH
THE ENGLISH
HAD POWER FOR CENTURIES
AFTER THE
NORMAN INVASION OF 1169

The word Pale comes from the Latin word palus, meaning a stake as used in a protective fence or palisade. The land within the Pale Ditch was entirely under the control of the English settlers and was known as the "maghery". In 1488 the Pale was defined as stretching from Dalkey to Dundalk, although the boundaries changed from time to time.

Landowners were required to construct a line of defence where their property touched the border, and every inhabitant was obliged to assist. The defence would to take the form of a double ditch, flanking a bank six feet high on one side, surmounted by a palisade. Remains of the Pale Ditch can still be seen in some areas, including Kilcross housing estate and Ballyogan (both shown here).

In this area of Dublin, the Pale Ditch was intended primarily to obstruct the theft of cattle during the periodic raids by the O'Byrnes and the O'Tooles of Wicklow. It is thought that these defence works were never completed. Only small sections remain today, partly due to destruction by landowners and by road works, etc.

...THAT WE HAVE REMNANTS OF THE PALEDITCH IN OUR AREA

?

One of the most famous bishops of Glendalough was St Laurence O'Toole, who was abbot from 1153 to 1162 when he became Archbishop of Dublin.

In 1214 King John united the dioceses of Glendalough and Dublin. From early times a pilgrimage to Glendalough was claimed to be the equivalent of one to Rome.

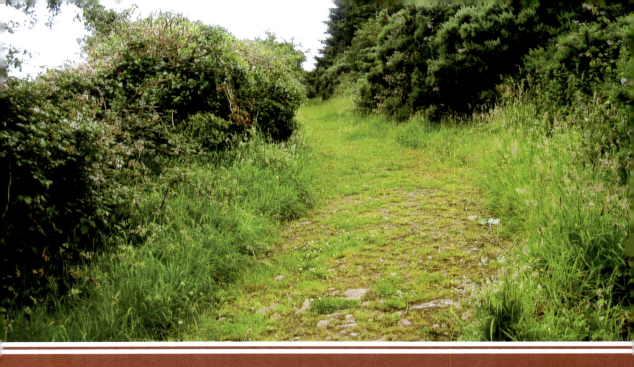

...THAT A TRACK LEADING PAST LEHAUNSTOWN AND THE ANCIENT CROSS AT TULLY AND OVER THE STEPPING STONES TO THE LOUGHLINSTOWN RIVER AT HERONFORD, IS THOUGHT TO BE PART OF THE PILGRIMAGE ROUTE FROM ST MARY'S ABBEY IN DUBLIN TO ST KEVIN'S MONASTERY IN GLENDALOUGH

THE WICKLOW WAY

The idea for a Wicklow Way was first suggested by J B Malone in 1966. It was laid out 12 years later by Cospoir (The National Sports Council). It runs south from Marlay Park to Clonegal in Co Carlow, and covers a distance of 131 kms. It leaves Dun Laoghaire-Rathdown just south of Glencullen Mountain after 18kms.

On the Wicklow Way walkers are led away from main roads and villages, and are taken through unspoilt country with many splendid views such as the Glencullen valley shown here.

The route is marked clearly by square black posts depicting a hiker with stick and rucksack and an arrow showing the direction to follow. The Way is popular with families out for a stroll as well as with serious hikers who tackle it in its entirety.

...THAT THE START OF THE WICKLOW WAY
IS IN MARLAY PARK

?

Two Rock Mountain is the most northerly summit of the Dublin – Wicklow Mountains. Its Irish name is Sliab Lecga or 'the mountain of the flagstones'. Somewhat confusingly the two rocks that give its name are not located at the summit of the mountain. A cairn, known as "the Fairy Castle", occupies this position. It is about 25m across and 2m high. It is likely that in the centre of the cairn is a small burial chamber.

The lower shoulder of Two Rock Mountain is called Three Rock. This is much better known because there is a path providing easy access to it. Three large rocks dominate its landscape, but from a distance it is more recognisable from the transmitter masts piercing the sky.

...THAT THE TWO ROCK MOUNTAIN, AT 536 METRES ABOVE SEA LEVEL, IS THE 381st HIGHEST MOUNTAIN IN IRELAND

One of the best-known archaeological sites in the country is the Carrickmines Castle site. The site was the subject of large-scale archaeological works during the construction of the M50 motorway.

During the construction of the motorway, adjustments were made to the design to provide access to a small section of the archaeological site. This area contains a revetted fosse and the window of a medieval gatehouse.

...THAT BY GOING UNDERNEATH THIS BRIDGE ON THE SLIP ROAD TO THE M50 AT THE CARRICKMINES INTERCHANGE YOU CAN VISIT THE PROTECTED EXCAVATION AREA OF CARRICKMINES CASTLE

?

Samuel Beckett was born in Cooldrinagh in Foxrock. He became a member of Carrickmines Golf Club while he was a student at Trinity College. In the Club's records it is recorded that he won the Carysfort Cup in 1925. To add some spice to his games of golf, he used to challenge the Club's Professional, James Barrett, with whom he was on easy terms, for the sum of seven shillings and sixpence.

Eoin O'Brien's book "The Beckett Country" highlights the many associations with this area in the works of Beckett. However, while there do not appear to be any references to the golf club in the writings, it is believed that in later life, as an antidote to insomnia, Beckett would play the holes at Carrickmines in his mind to induce relaxation and sleep.

...THAT CARRICKMINES GOLF CLUB WAS SAMUEL BECKETT'S GOLF CLUB

Bhí sé ina bhall le linn dó bheith ina mhac léinn i gColáiste na Tríonóide agus tá sé ar taifead gur bhuaigh sé Corn Dhún Carúin i 1925. Le spreagadh a chur sna cluichí gailf ba nós leis dúshlán Ghalfaire Gairmiúil an Chlub James Barrett, fear a mbíodh caidreamh maith aige leis, a thabhairt, agus geall de sheacht scilling agus sé phingin a chur leis go mbéarfadh sé an bua air. Ní dhealraíonn sé go bhfuil aon tagairt déanta don chlub gailf i scríbhinní Samuel Beckett ach tá sé ráite, go n-imríodh sé poill ghalfchúrsa Charraig Mhaighin ina intinn istoíche níos deireanaí ina shaol d'fhonn a smaointí a mhealladh chun codlata.

...GO N-IMRÍODH SAMUEL BECKETT I GCLUB GAILF
CHARRAIG MHAIGHIN

?

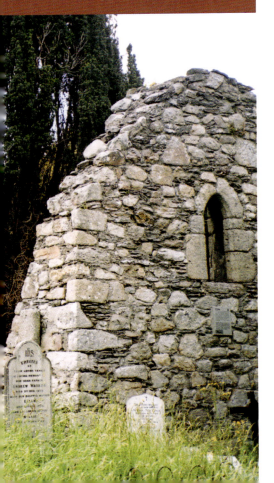

This tower is at the south – west corner of the church, and its remains are just 1.83m high. It is impossible to know if the tower was ever completed and, if it was completed, why or when it either fell or was demolished. However, it is an indication of the former importance of the church at Rathmichael. The site appears to be dedicated to St Michael, the patron saint of seafarers, while the area was also near an important pilgrim route to Glendalough.

The tower probably dates from the 9th century, and is one of only four in Dublin. According to legend there was an underground passage leading from the tower to the sea and a piper, who descended into the passage playing sweet music, was said never to have been seen again.

However, the nickname comes from a much later era. After many years the church graveyard became full and space was needed for new burials. Neglected areas were cleared of ancient remains, which were then thrown into the tower. People looking in over the walls would have been able to see bones, most notably the skulls.

...THAT THIS BASE OF A ROUND TOWER BESIDE THE OLD CHURCH OF RATHMICHAEL IS KNOWN AS THE "SKULL HOLE"

?

The story goes that, some time before 1837, the cross was coveted by Sir George Cockburn of Shanganagh Castle who collected antiquities.

A pamphlet, published in 1906 by the Shankill Branch of the Gaelic League states "General Cockburn sent two men with a horse and cart to steal the cross. They chose a beautiful moonlit night but no sooner had they stirred the cross than the wind rose and the rain fell heavily. However, they persevered and put the cross on the cart. The previously willing horse now kicked and refused to pull, so had to be removed from his harness. The men themselves then drew the cart and cross back to Shanganagh. A serious accident happened to one man unloading the cross and some members of their families came to misfortune!"

In about 1910 the cross was re-placed in Rathmichael Lane where we see it today. This lane would once have led up to Rathmichael old church and the cross may have marked the entry to church property.

...THE CURIOUS STORY ATTACHED TO THIS LITTLE
GRANITE CROSS IN RATHMICHAEL

?

The cross is located on the grounds of Stepaside public golf course. Many golfers searching for lost golf balls have been confronted by this curious object. It lies beside a holy well (now dry) and it is rather forbidding in aspect. One side of the cross bears a man's figure with his head sunk on his shoulders. The arms of this "hunchbacked" figure seem to come from behind his ears, the hands are in front of the body and the legs hang from the hips with feet pointed outwards. On the other side there appears to be a circle and mouldings, though some people claim to make out a figure. The cross may have been associated with a nearby church.

The surrounding townland was originally called Ballymochain and the cross and well were dedicated to St Caoin, brother of St Kevin of Glendalough. His feast day was 1 May when pilgrims visited the cross and well. This date is also the feast of St James. Which suggests that even after St Caoin was forgotten the day was not. St James took over and gave his name to the townland, cross and well.

It should be noted that there is also speculation that this is not a holy cross at all but instead a "sheela-na-gig" or fertility symbol.

...THAT THERE IS A STRANGE LITTLE CROSS ON AN ANCIENT LANEWAY NOW SURROUNDED BY THE STEPASIDE PUBLIC GOLF COURSE IN JAMESTOWN

?

OUR LADY OF THE WAYSIDE

O LADY OF THE WAYSIDE
TAKE ME BY THE HAND
AND FOR THE SAKE OF
THE CHILD YOU BEAR
IN YOUR ARMS,
LEAD ME SAFELY TO
THE END OF THE ROAD

The church was dedicated by Archbishop Byrne in 1929, on the centenary of both Catholic Emancipation and the establishment of the parish of Sandyford. The name came as inspiration to Canon Kelly, the parish priest of Sandyford, when he saw the miraculous picture of the Madonna Della Strada (the Lady of the Ways) in Rome. The church cost £3,368 and the architects were Kaye, Ross & Hendy.

The church's unique design and picturesque setting make it a very popular choice for weddings.

...THAT THE CHURCH OF OUR LADY OF THE WAYSIDE, KILTERNAN, IS CONSTRUCTED FROM WOOD

?

Much of our landscape was shaped and moulded by glaciers thousands of years ago. The Scalp is one of the most striking landscape features that was formed during the last Ice Age. It is a channel that was cut by immense amounts of glacial melt water which drained the great ice sheet covering the midlands of Ireland. As the ice retreated, the Scalp contained a surface river that flowed south from the margin of the ice sheet and carried sands and gravel into Glacial Lake at Enniskerry which, in turn, drained out through the Glen of the Downs!

...THAT THE SCALP WAS GOUGED OUT BY A RIVER THAT RAN UNDERNEATH AN ICE SHEET

?

I gcaitheamh na hOighearaoise rug an abhainn léi uisce leáite gan chuimse agus í ag draenáil na hoighearchlúide ollmhóire a chlúdaigh Lár Tíre na hÉireann. Is é méid agus neart na huisce a ghearr amach an cainéal. Níos deireanaí nuair a chúlaigh an oighear, bhí abhainn dromchla ag rith ó dheas ó imeall na hoighearchlúide ag breith gaineamh agus gairbhéal léi isteach i Loch Áth na Sceire, a dhraenáil ar a sheal trí Ghleann Dá Ghrua.

...GUR ABHAINN A RITH FAOI OIGHEARCHLÚID A GHEARR AN SCAILP AS CRAICEANN NA TALÚN

?

The skeletal remains of over 100 Giant Deer have been discovered at Ballybetagh Bog near Glencullen. The Giant Deer was one of the largest deer to have ever lived. This magnificent male is housed in the Museum Building in Trinity College. Megaloceros giganteus, or the so – called Irish Elk was a victim of the Ice Age and disappeared from Ireland around 10,500 years ago. These fantastic creatures roamed the lowlands of central and eastern Ireland. The males were most impressive, standing 7ft high at the shoulder and carrying antlers which measured up to 12 feet from antler tip to antler tip. Being antlers, not horns, these were shed and regrown each year. The females were equally tall, but had no antlers.

...THAT BALLYBETAGH BOG, JUST EAST OF GLENCULLEN, IS THE MOST IMPORTANT SITE IN IRELAND FOR THE RECOVERY OF FOSSIL REMAINS OF THE GIANT IRISH DEER

?

The castle is of interest as it is situated on an important highway of medieval times. This was referred to in a deed of 1243 naming "the great, straight road to Shankill". A large annual fair used to be held in the adjoining fields in medieval times. It was held on 10 October.

The origin of the name "Puck" is not known. It may have to do with a fairy piper, said to hop from rock to rock playing his pipe until he disappears down the souterrain! Or it may refer to the goats that were once found nearby.

The castle is famous chiefly for the story that it was visited by James II when his army was camped in neighbouring Lehaunstown, when fleeing after the Battle of the Boyne. Peter Lawless was said to be in residence at that time, and it is rumoured that King James left a very generous gift of silver in the castle.

...THAT PUCK'S CASTLE IN RATHMICHAEL IS NOT A
TRUE CASTLE BUT MORE A FORTIFIED DWELLING

?

POST OFFICE KILTERNAN

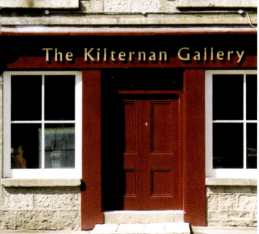

Acquired by Edward Willis in 1890 it operated as a post office, grocery and hardware store. For a century it was the social focal point for the Kilternan and Glencullen area. The photographs of the interior were taken on the last day of the functioning of the post office and shop, 26 June 1990. Mr Eric Willis, son of Edward Willis, died on the evening after.

Today, the Willis family have carefully preserved the facade and shop front, and use the old shop as an art gallery.

...THAT KILTERNAN POST OFFICE (NOW THE KILTERNAN GALLERY) WAS ONE OF THE LAST "OLD WORLD" COUNTRY POST OFFICES IN THE COUNTY

?

Bodysnatching was, at one time, so prevalent that relatives and friends of someone who had recently died used to watch over the grave for several days. This tower in Cruagh cemetery was actually provided for the purpose.

Bodysnatching was considered necessary as, before the Anatomy Act of 1832, the only legal supply of corpses for the anatomical education of medical students was the bodies of criminals sentenced by the courts to "Death and Dissection".

This did not provide enough subjects for the medical students' needs so the schools turned to employing "bodysnatchers" who raided graveyards, removing recent burials. This crime was considered only a misdemeanour and carried merely a fine or short term of imprisonment.

The bodysnatchers used to enter the cemetery at night carrying wooden spades for quiet digging. They were careful when removing the corpse to leave behind all clothing and jewellery as taking these would be a felony, which was considered a much graver crime.

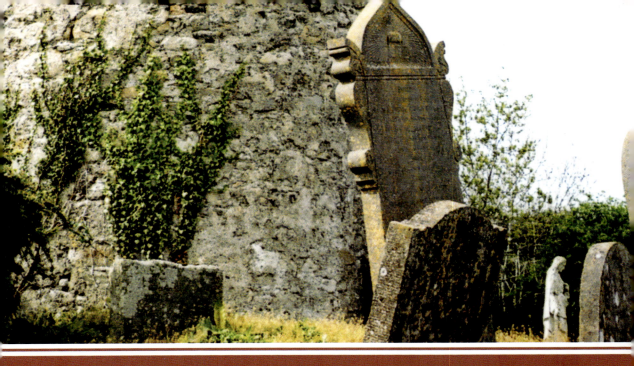

...WHY BODYSNATCHERS WERE NECESSARY

In 1845 there was a proposal to build a railway line from Harcourt Street station to Enniskerry. The line was intended to run through Dundrum and Stepaside and then through the Scalp and on to the picturesque Wicklow village. The project never came to fruition, and the photograph shown here would never happen.

Construction on a line between Bray and Enniskerry was started in the 1880s, but this was never completed. The track was subsequently taken up and sold to pay off debts. However, today some stonework can still be seen beside the road from the N11 to Enniskerry.

...THAT STEPASIDE NEARLY HAD A RAILWAY STATION

KILGOBBIN CASTLE

Kilgobbin Castle is believed to have been built by the powerful Walsh family in the 15th century, and they are recorded as having lived in the castle for many years.

Some people believe the castle is haunted by a man wearing armour who walks around the nearby cottages at night. Also it is rumoured that a woman goes into the castle to collect something golden in colour and comes back out again. That story links closely with the other rumour about the castle, namely that there was buried treasure found there.

...THAT KILGOBBIN CASTLE, KNOWN FOR ITS HISTORY AS A PALE CASTLE AND FOR THE BATTLE THAT TOOK PLACE THERE IN 1642, ALSO HAS A MYSTERIOUS SIDE

?

It has nothing to do with socks or tights. Instead it marked the start of the old Military Road crossing the mountains south of Dublin. The name refers to the soldiers "stocking" up on supplies at this point, before they marched south.

The Military Road is a route through the Wicklow Mountains built in 1800 to open up the mountains to the English military after the 1798 Rebellion. It took nine years to build and is 43 miles long.

There were four barracks along the route, Glencree, Laragh, Drumgoff and Aughavannagh. None remained as a barracks for more than 30 years.

These paths through Massy Woods in Rathfarnham are part of the old Military Road.

...HOW "STOCKING LANE" GOT ITS NAME

A triangulation station is a fixed surveying point used in the preparation of maps. By providing fixed location points they allow other locations to be accurately mapped. Triangulation began in Britain in 1783. In 1824 it was decided that a 6" to the mile map of Ireland was needed for land taxing.

The first triangulation station in Ireland was on Divis Mountain outside Belfast. One of the main problems for the early Irish map makers was what one called the "inveterate haze and fogginess" in Ireland that made observation of distant stations difficult. In 1825 Thomas Drummond of the Ordnance Survey improved the technology with a "limelight" for night observation and a reflector for daytime. These allowed Divis Mountain to be observed from Scotland. It became the first fixed point, the first triangulation station, in Ireland.

Originally the markers for the triangulation stations were buried, as they were liable to be attacked, stolen or damaged. In later years the markers were placed above ground and made permanent in nature. The Triangulation Station shown here is on Mount Pelier beside the Hellfire Club. There is another, in better condition, on top of the Two Rock Mountain. There used to be a third at ground level on Carrickgollogan but it has disappeared.

didyouknow...

BETWEEN THE MOUNTAINS AND THE SEA

?

CHURCH OF THE ASCENSION OF THE LORD

Liam McCormick was the most eminent of modernist Irish church architects and is highly regarded internationally. McCormick was born in Derry in 1916 and he studied architecture in the University of Liverpool. Renowned for the innovative and imaginative nature of his work, he designed many of the modern Catholic churches in the north-west, especially in Donegal and Derry. The best known one is St. Aengus's in Burt, County Donegal.

The Church of the Ascension is one of only three of McCormick's in the Dublin area. The church at Balally opened in 1982. It is described as "a large red-brick rotunda linked to a smaller circular sacristy, defensive looking in its introversion with large blank walls". It exhibits many of the characteristics of McCormick's work such as the curved seating within the circular form and the unusual use of lighting, in this case from low-level windows.

The design of the Church of the Ascension was inspired by Eero Saarinen's MIT chapel in Boston.

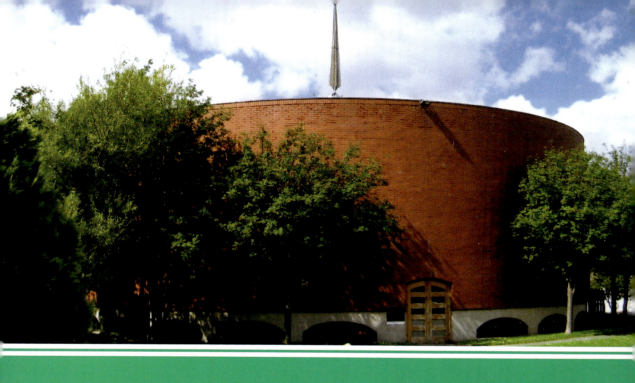

...THAT THE CHURCH OF THE ASCENSION OF THE LORD IN BALALLY WAS DESIGNED BY LIAM MCCORMICK

?

WILLIAM DARGAN

William Dargan (1799-1867) was the most famous Irish businessman of Victorian Ireland. He built many of the country's railways, including the Dublin-Kingstown and the Dublin-Bray (Harcourt Street) lines. He organised and financed the Great Industrial Exhibition of 1853, and is honoured by a statue that is now in front of the National Gallery on the site of the exhibition.

Dargan enlarged the original house at Mount Anville and added the tower as a belvedere. Queen Victoria, who visited the Exhibition, also paid a visit to his house. When the Exhibition was dismantled, Dargan retrieved some features. He re-erected the gates at his garden in Mount Anville. The fountain is now in front of Bewley's Hotel, Ballsbridge.

...THAT MOUNT ANVILLE WAS THE HOME OF WILLIAM DARGAN

?

First, William Dargan, as railway contractor, built the Harcourt Street Line (Dublin to Bray) which opened in 1853-4. Later, in 1864, he became Chairman of the Dublin and Wicklow Railway Company. Secondly, Dargan also lived nearby in Mount Anville (see adjacent panel) and so Dundrum railway station was his local station for journeys to his office. This association may help explain why there is something special about its architectural qualities.

It is surely fitting that his station building, a listed building, which, as shown here, was recently damaged by fire, will soon be restored.

...WHY IT IS DOUBLY FITTING THAT THE LUAS BRIDGE AT DUNDRUM IS CALLED THE WILLIAM DARGAN BRIDGE

?

ST HELEN'S HOUSE

St Helen's House, formerly Seamount, was built around 1754 in a beautiful location overlooking Dublin Bay. In the 19th century the house was extended by Viscount Gough to the designs of the architect John McCurdy, while the famous garden designer Ninian Niven laid out the formal terrace garden. Later Sir John Nutting remodelled the house, which today boasts a marble hall, fine stucco ceilings, painted panelling and well-proportioned rooms.

In 1925 the house was bought by the Christian Brothers to be their Provincial Residence and Novitiate. Following its sale by the Christian Brothers in 1988, St Helen's suffered from vandalism and the threat of demolition. However, in 1994, following a public campaign, the house and gardens were registered under the 1987 National Monuments (Amendment) Act which provided the appropriate recognition of its significance. Today Saint Helen's is a hotel.

...THAT THE FUTURE OF ST HELEN'S HOUSE (NOW THE RADISSON HOTEL) ON THE STILLORGAN ROAD WAS SECURED THROUGH A PUBLIC CAMPAIGN

?

THE MANOR MILL LAUNDRY
DUNDRUM, CO. DUBLIN.

tablished   in 18

ealthful   Large
Country   of
ituation;   skilled h

undance   well
    of
ure Soft   ventila

Water;   Workro

ge Drying   Applian
   and   complet
leaching
Ground.   every rea

The Vans visit all parts of Dublin and Suburbs, Blackrock, Kingst
lkey, and (in the summer months) Bray.
Price Lists on application to the Manager.

Water power was the original attraction. It is likely that the millpond in Dundrum is medieval in origin. There is written mention of a corn mill in 1602, and around 1800 of a paper mill and an iron works. The millpond survived reasonably intact until the early 2000s. It has now been turned into a water feature associated with the new shopping centre, "Dundrum Town Centre", and has lost virtually all of its character as a millpond, with the exception of the granite mill dam and spillway, and other minor features.

The mill house shown here is another reminder of the past: a 1762 map shows what appears to be this house and there is another reference to it in 1843. In the second half of the 19th century the Manor Mill Laundry was established and it continued in operation until 1942. It is now a private residence.

...THAT THE MILLPOND IN DUNDRUM TOWN CENTRE IS
EVIDENCE OF INDUSTRIAL ACTIVITIES ON THIS SITE
SINCE THE 14TH CENTURY

?

THE BOTTLE TOWER CHURCHTOWN

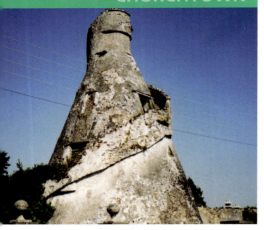

The winter of 1741-2 was particularly hard, and being long before the days of social welfare and cold – weather payments, the poor suffered terribly. To alleviate their poverty, and in the belief that reward should not be given except in return for labour, many landlords provided work by building follies. The Bottle Tower is thought to have been built in imitation of "The Wonderful Barn" in Leixlip despite the fact that the barn was finished in 1743, a year after the Bottle Tower was built.

The Churchtown Bottle Tower, in spite of being a folly, was used to store grain. There is a smaller companion tower beside it which was used as a pigeon house. Any spilt grain fed the pigeons and the owners would have benefited by the supply of both eggs and meat. The rings on the dovecote prevented rats from entering, and also gave a landing stage for the birds.

...THAT THE BOTTLE TOWER IN CHURCHTOWN IS A FOLLY

?

This photo (left) shows the "Hermitage" in the grounds of St Enda's Park in Rathfarnham. It dates from the late 18th – early 19th centuries. A "hermit" would have been engaged occasionally to peer out from it at the visitors! Also in St Enda's, another folly, the Gothic – style rustic gateway (right) could only have served as a decorative feature on the walk around the grounds. "Emmet's Fort", in a corner of St Enda's, is built in the shape of a five-pointed star, and consists of four oddly – shaped rooms and a tiny staircase. It may have been intended as a play area for children.

...THAT A "FOLLY" IS A STRUCTURE BUILT FOR PLEASURE HAVING NO OBVIOUS PRACTICAL FUNCTION

?

AIR RAID SHELTER CABINTEELY HOUSE

During the Second World War this shelter was built by the McGrath family in the grounds of Cabinteely House. Originally the entrance had a blast wall in front of it. It was never put into effective use although German planes did bomb Glasthule in 1940. These "beehive" structures were designed by the Irish Defence Forces to resist the blast of a 500 pound bomb exploding as close as 50 feet away. Each could accommodate up to 6 people.

Cabinteely House was built in 1769 by Robert Nugent, Lord Clare, who was related to the Byrne family who owned the demesne. The walls of the estate took five years to build. The house, modified in Victorian times, was bought by Joe McGrath (of Irish Hospital Sweepstakes fame) in 1933. His family presented it to Dublin County Council in 1969.

...THAT THIS IS AN AIR RAID SHELTER

?

THE YEATS SISTERS

Susan Mary (Lily) Yeats (1866-1949) and Elizabeth Corbet (Lolly) Yeats (1868-1940) were the sisters of William Butler and Jack Butler Yeats. They lived at Gurteen Dhas, near the Bottle Tower in Churchtown. Although overshadowed by their brothers they were prominent in the Irish Arts and Crafts Movement. Lily specialised in embroidery and Lolly in printing on a hand press.

In 1902 they joined Dun Emer Industries, on the Sandyford Road, founded by Evelyn Gleeson. Later, in 1908, they founded Cuala Industries in a two-roomed cottage overlooking Milltown Golf Club. They worked in Churchtown until 1923 when they, and "the young Irish girls" who helped them, moved to other premises. There are four pieces of their embroidered work hanging in St Naithi's Church in Dundrum. The Yeats sisters are buried in the adjacent graveyard.

CUALA INDUSTRIES, LTD.,
CHURCHTOWN, DUNDRUM,
CO. DUBLIN.

EMBROIDERY   -   LILY YEATS.
HAND PRESS   -   ELIZABETH C. YEATS.

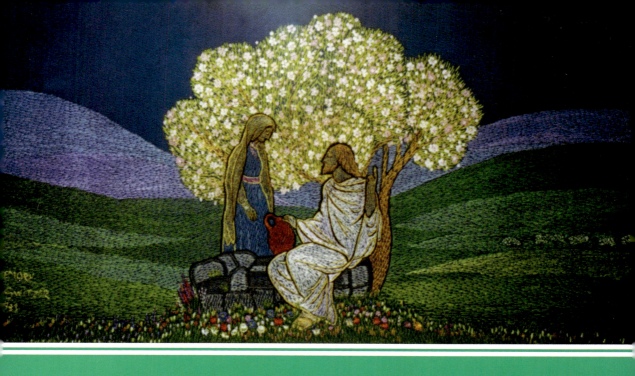

...THAT DUNDRUM HAS CONNECTIONS WITH
THE YEATS FAMILY

?

THE DUBLIN WICKLOW RAILWAY COMPANY

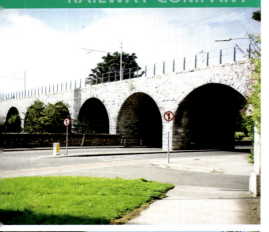

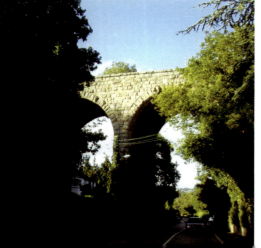

When the Harcourt Street railway line opened, the journey to Bray took 35 minutes. On its journey the train passed over the Dodder river on the Milltown Viaduct (top image). This was built in 1849 and is known as the "Nine Arches". A second viaduct was built in 1853 and crosses the Bride's Glen, near Loughlinstown (bottom image). The journey from Dublin to Bray passed through a number of stations. The Stillorgan Station (opposite) was probably designed by the famous railway engineer, William Dargan. Today it is a private house.

The Harcourt Street line was closed on 1 January 1959. It has recently been replaced by the Luas tramline which runs between Harcourt Street and the Stillorgan Reservoir. Work is currently underway to extend the Luas line southwards but this part of the route will not follow the original line of the railway.

...THAT THE DUBLIN WICKLOW RAILWAY COMPANY OPENED THE RAILWAY LINE FROM HARCOURT STREET STATION TO BRAY IN 1854

LEOPARDSTOWN RACECOURSE

Leopardstown Racecourse was opened in August 1888 and is modelled on Sandown Racecourse in England. It caters for all three types of horse races: flat racing, hurdling and steeplechasing. Each year it hosts some of the most important races in the Irish calendar.

Flat racing is English in origin, but steeplechasing is Irish. It began in 1752 when two riders settled an argument over whose horse was best by racing to a distant church steeple jumping all obstacles on the way. Hurdle races began in England when, in 1791, the Prince Regent had a disagreement with the Jockey Club. He moved his court to Brighton and held his own race meetings on the Downs where shepherds enclosed their sheep in hurdles. Some friends of the Prince made fences from the hurdles to enliven their races.

...THAT THERE HAS BEEN RACING AT LEOPARDSTOWN
FOR OVER 120 YEARS

?

DEANSGRANGE CEMETERY

Most people are familiar with the many famous figures buried at Dublin's Glasnevin Cemetery, but Deansgrange Cemetery has its own fascinating story to tell through the graves of those buried there.

Deansgrange Cemetery was opened in 1865 and now there are over 150,000 buried within its grounds.

Among these are the inventor of the pneumatic tyre John Boyd Dunlop, taoisigh Sean Lemass and John A. Costello, James Byrne the famous newspaper seller from Dún Laoghaire, astronomer Howard Grubb, victims of the MV Leinster and the 1894 Dún Laoghaire lifeboat disaster, Nora Connolly the daughter of James Connolly, comedian and actor Dermot Morgan, Count John McCormack, Nobel Prize – winning physicist Ernest Walton, doctor, TD and revolutionary Kathleen Lynn, writer Alice Stopford Green, architect Raymond McGrath, composer John Larchet and many, many more.

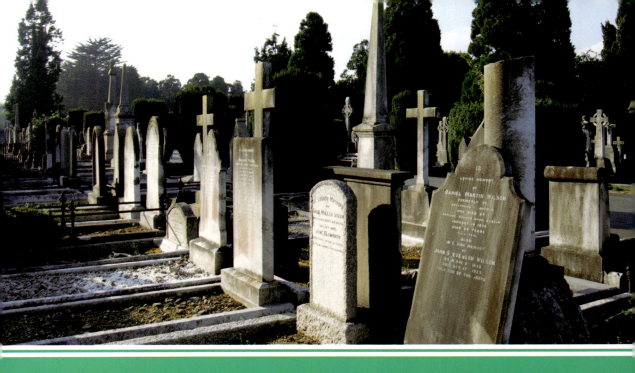

...THAT DEANSGRANGE CEMETERY IS THE RESTING PLACE OF MANY IMPORTANT, FAMOUS AND INTERESTING PEOPLE

TANEY BELLS

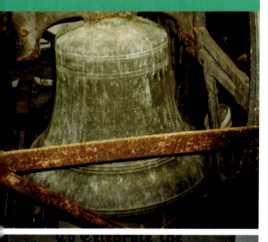

**To celebrate the
Third Millennium of Faith**

The eight bells from St. George's Church,
(closed 1990)
were installed in Christ Church, Taney
through the generosity of:

**PARISHIONERS OF TANEY
THE PARISH OF ST. GEORGE AND ST. THOMAS
TREVOR BROOKS & FAMILY
THE MILLAR FAMILY
OVEREND FAMILY TRUST OF AIRFIELD
THE NATIONAL MILLENNIUM COMMITTEE
CANON A.W.F. ORR In Memoriam
ELIZABETH CURTIS In Memoriam**

**THE IRISH ASSOCIATION OF CHANGE RINGERS
THE COMMUNITY OF DUNDRUM AND BEYOND**

The bells were originally in St George's Church in Hardwicke Street where Joyce would have heard them. He wrote; "A creek and a dark whirr in the air high up. The bells of George's church. They tolled the hour: loud dark iron. Heigh ho! Heigh ho! Heigh ho!"

When St George's closed in April 1990, the bells were carefully dismantled and removed to safe storage. Canon D Sinnamon of Taney Parish helped with the dismantling and was offered the bells for his church.

It was hoped to install the bells in Taney in time to ring in the 21st century. Thanks to generous public response to fundraising, and a huge effort from the Taney Bell committee ,the goal was achieved. The bells arrived at the beginning of December and were installed in the tower in time for the millennium celebrations. Each bell has its own inscription e.g. "Universal Benevolence" and "Peace and Prosperity to Ireland". On the tenor bell is inscribed the following:

"We were all cast by Thomas Mears of London and presented to the Parish Church of St George's, Dublin by Francis Johnston, Architect of said Church and Mrs Anne Johnston, his wife. 1828."

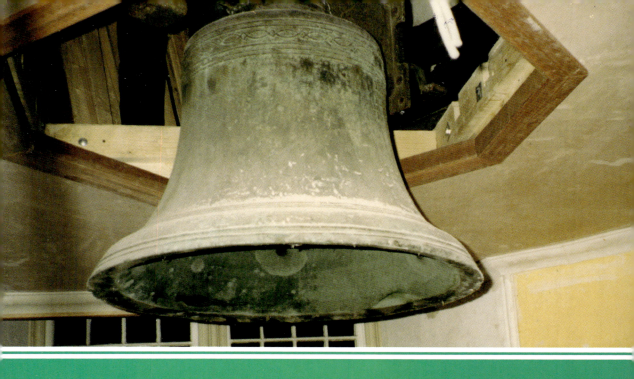

...THAT THE BELLS IMMORTALISED BY JAMES JOYCE
IN HIS WRITINGS CAN BE HEARD IN CHRIST CHURCH
AND TANEY, DUNDRUM

"Goats' milk has been observed to have affected some remarkable cures of consumption where cows' and asses' milk had failed," wrote Dr John Rutty in 1772.

Dundrum, and the surrounding district, was especially celebrated as an area for invalids to visit and take lodgings. It was described as…"the fashionable resort of invalids for the purpose of drinking goats' whey. At early hours of the morning numerous jaunting-cars convey from the city large parties of visitors to partake of that sanative beverage, amidst the reviving scenery over which the animals have browsed" (from Brewer, "Beauties of Ireland", 1826).

Goatstown, by its name, must have had a special reputation arising from the quality – or the quantity – of its goats. One may still partake of a (different) "sanative beverage" here…

...THAT THE GOAT AT GOATSTOWN IS A REMINDER OF THE TIME, TWO HUNDRED YEARS AGO, WHEN PHYSICIANS RECOMMENDED THEIR PATIENTS TO DRINK GOATS' MILK

?

Grandad Campbell moved to Dundrum in 1920 after his shoe repair shop in Parliament Street burned down. He had a contract to repair the boots of the military; later there was major contract work for the repair of boots and shoes for nearby Dundrum Mental Hospital. Today the third and fourth generations work in the shop which now repairs footwear and all types of bags as well as selling a variety of leather goods.

At one time it operated a collection and delivery service (by bicycle). However, on occasions if the front door was left unlocked at night and customers called they would collect their shoes and leave the payment on the counter. Ah, times past!

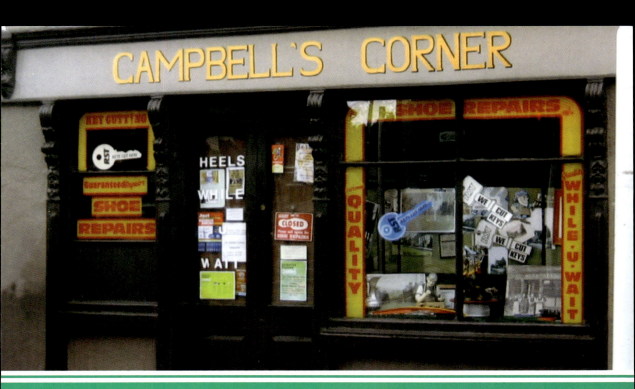

...THAT THE CAMPBELLS HAVE BEEN REPAIRING SHOES HERE AT CAMPBELL'S CORNER IN DUNDRUM SINCE 1920

PACKHORSE BRIDGE

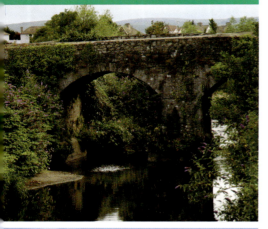

The Packhorse Bridge dates from medieval times. It is a two – arch bridge with a central pier in the river. Although known as the Packhorse Bridge, it may also have carried wheeled traffic, as there is a pedestrian refuge on the western side. For many years it was the only bridge across the Dodder: there was a ford nearby which took most of the wheeled traffic.

...THAT THE PACKHORSE BRIDGE OVER THE RIVER DODDER IN MILLTOWN IS THE OLDEST BRIDGE SOUTH OF THE RIVER LIFFEY AND IS POSSIBLY THE OLDEST ONE IN THE DUBLIN AREA

WILLIAM SEALY GOSSET

William Sealy Gosset was born in Canterbury and educated at Oxford. He moved to Dublin in 1899 and was employed as a scientist in the Guinness brewery (photo of Guinness bewers in 1923 shown here). He lived at Woodlands on Rochestown Avenue (1909-1915) and Holly Park House, Blackrock (1915-1935), now the site of Holly Park School. As part of his employment at Guinness, Gosset addressed many problems associated with statistical sampling. Given the nature of his work he was especially concerned with the difficulties associated with small sampling in the brewery. Addressing this issue he wrote what is regarded as a classic paper of modern statistics called "The Probable Error of a Mean". This paper fundamentally changed an important area of statistics.

However, Gosset's name is not associated with this breakthrough because another researcher at Guinness had previously published a paper containing trade secrets of the Guinness brewery. To prevent further disclosure of confidential information, Guinness prohibited its employees from publishing any papers, regardless of the contained information. Therefore, Gosset published under the pseudonym "Student" and his breakthrough in statistics was, and still is, called the "Student t-distribution".

...THAT A GREAT STATISTICIAN LIVED IN BLACKROCK

?

KEVIN O'HIGGINS

Kevin O'Higgins was from Laois and was one of the leading figures in post-Independence Ireland. He was a TD for Laois and was a supporter of the Treaty. In 1922 he was Minister for Finance and then Minister for Home Affairs. He was one of the key figures in the Cumann na nGaedheal government.

On Sunday 10 July, 1927 O'Higgins left his home at Dunamase House, Cross Avenue, Booterstown. He was walking to mid-day mass alone when three gunmen attacked him near the junction of Cross Avenue and Booterstown Avenue. He died shortly afterwards. His assassination shocked the country. It is believed that O'Higgin's was assassinated in reprisal for his support of Civil War executions of republican prisoners, including Rory O'Connor who had been best man at his wedding. O'Connor's execution was in reprisal for the assassination of Sean Hales, TD.

O'Higgins was just 35 years old at the time of his death. He was buried in Glasnevin Cemetery. His funeral cortege was over three miles long.

...THAT KEVIN O'HIGGIN'S WAS ASSASSINATED IN BOOTERSTOWN

?

The Wright brothers' first flight took place in 1903 while the first flight in Ireland was at Newcastle beach in Wicklow in 1909. However, the first chance for the public to appreciate the spectacle of human flight took place on the grounds of Leopardstown Racecourse on 29 and 30 August, 1910. According to one report "for the first time, there were seen men careering far beyond racing speed over Leopardstown Racecourse; between old Killiney Hill with its Obelisk and Ballycorus Tower…"

Three of the most famous aviators of the day took part in the display. Captain Bertram Dickson, who was a key figure in the establishment of the British Air Force, gave a demonstration of "Circular Flying". Armstrong Drexel, who held the eighth pilots' licence issued in the United States of America, gave a display of "high flying". Cecil Grace performed in his Farman Biplane – he died just four months later when flying across the English Channel.

...THAT LEOPARDSTOWN RACECOURSE WAS THE
LOCATION FOR IRELAND'S FIRST AVIATION MEETING

MOUNT MERRION ESTATE

When the FitzWilliam family abandoned their castle at Merrion in 1710 they built a new residence at the elevated site of Mount Merrion. However, the family did not live there for long and rented out the house. Among the tenants in 1789 was John Fitzgibbon, the Lord Chancellor of Ireland. The lodge of Mount Merrion still exists today and is a community centre.

The Mount Merrion Estate was extensive and included the land known as "Deer Park". Today Deerpark is a public park the boundaries of which correspond exactly to the walled woodland area laid out with radial paths shown on the earliest map. Other remnant landscape features of the estate are Mount Merrion Avenue and Cross Avenue, shown here. These long, straight avenues are unusual in the city and they were laid out as formal avenues by Richard Viscount FitzWilliam when he landscaped the estate. One of the gates to the FitzWilliam Estate was taken from its original location at the Booterstown Avenue end of Cross Avenue and re-erected at the entrance to Willow Park school. Extensive sections of the original estate wall still exist in the area.

...THAT MOUNT MERRION AVENUE AND CROSS AVENUE IN BLACKROCK WERE ONCE PART OF A HUGE 18TH CENTURY LANDSCAPING PLAN

Nuair a d'fhág teaghlach FitzWilliam a gcaisleán ag Muirfean i 1710 thóg siad teach nua ar shuíomh ardaithe Chnoc Mhuirfean. Ní fada a bhí cónaí ag an teaghlach ann áfach agus lig siad an teach amach ar chíos – ar na tionóntaí a bhí ann i 1789 bhí John Fitzgibbon Tiarna Seansiléar na hÉireann. Tá lóiste Chnoc Mhuirfean fós ann inniu agus is ionad pobail é. B'fhairsing an dúiche í eastát Chnoc Mhuirfean a chuimsigh na tailte a thugtar Páirc na bhFianna orthu – sa lá atá inniu ann is páirc phoiblí Páirc na bhFianna agus cuimsíonn sí limistéar faoi choill a fhreagraíonn go beacht leis an limistéar coillearnach imfhálaithe le conairí leagtha amach go gathach a léirítear ar na léarscálanna is luaithe. Iarsmaí eile de ghnéithe tírdhreacha an eastáit is ea Ascaill Chnoc Mhuirfean agus Ascaill na Croise - atá léirithe anseo. Is neamhghnách ascaillí fada díreacha mar seo a fheiceáil sa chathair agus is mar ascaillí foirmeálta a leag Richard Bíocúnta FitzWilliam amach iad nuair a thírdhreachtaigh sé an t-eastát. Aistríodh ceann de gheataí bunaidh Eastát FitzWilliam ón áit a raibh sé i dtosach ag ceann Ascaill Bhaile an Bhóthair d'Ascaill na Croise agus tógadh in athuair é ag an mbealach isteach chuig scoil Pháirc na Sailí.

...GO RAIBH ASCAILL CHNOC MHUIRFEAN AGUS ASCAILL NA CROISE INA GCODANNA TRÁTH DÁ RAIBH DE PHLEAN OLLMHÓR TÍRDHREACHA AN OCHTÚ HAOIS DÉAG

?

MARLAY PARK POND

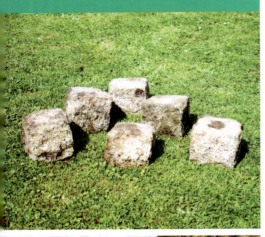

It is a small, shallow pond bounded on one side by the high wall of the coachyard and on the road side by a low stone wall. The two ends are left open.

The reason for the gaps was to allow carriages returning from muddy journeys to drive in one end and out the other, thus washing their wheels before turning into the yard.

Nowadays, the two ends have been fenced off for safety reasons and the pond itself has become muddier than the roads and is full of pond life.

Other reminders of the days of horse-drawn traffic are jostle stones to protect corners of walls from turning carriages, and cobblestones which gave a grip to horses' hooves. Cobblestones are correctly known as setts and are actually perfect granite cubes.

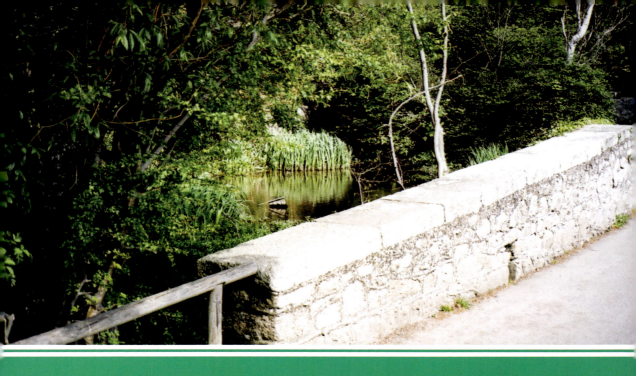

...THAT THE SMALL POND JUST OUTSIDE THE OLD COACHYARD IN MARLAY PARK HAD A SPECIAL PURPOSE

?

There are two tall crosses near Tully Church. Tully is known in Irish as 'tulach na n-Epscop', 'the hill of the bishops' and was an important religious centre. The western cross at Tully, which may have marked the boundary of the church, is believed to date from the 12th century. The cross is 2.2 metres high and, according to arcaeologist Chris Corlett, it depicts a figure of a bearded bishop (possibly St Laurence O'Toole) wearing a full length garment and holding a crozier.

The east cross was placed high on a granite plinth in 1987. It is a plain Celtic cross with little evidence of decoration, and is in better condition than the west cross.

A third tall cross in this area can be found at Kilgobbin. It shows the crucifixion in low relief on one side and on the other a figure clothed in a long garment to the ankles.

...THAT THERE ARE A NUMBER OF ANCIENT CROSSES
IN DÚN LAOGHAIRE

?

THIS STONE
WAS ERECTED BY
MARGARET LOUISA SMITHSON
IN LOVING REMEMBRANCE
OF HER BROTHER IN LAW
JOHN SMITHSON
WHO DEPARTED THIS L... APRIL 24. 1879
AGED 0

COME UNTO ME ... L YE
THAT ARE WEARY AND HEAVY LADEN
AND I ...LL GI E YOU REST

I HALL G TO HIM
UT HE SHALL NOT RETURN TO ME

ALSO
ANNIE M P SMITHSON
DIED 21ST FEBRUARY 1948,
AGED 74 YEARS.
"REST IN PEACE"

The Weldons of Tibradden

Annie M. P. Smithson

The Weldons of Tibradden follows the fortunes of three generations of the Weldon family beginning in the 1870s and ending in 1935. It is a fascinating story of success, courage, love and betrayal.

Annie Smithson was a district nurse in Rathfarnham for many years. She was also the most successful romantic novelist of her day. She wrote 19 novels, including one called "The Weldons of Tibradden". She became an ardent nationalist during the War of Independence and later became the secretary of The Irish Nurses Union.

Her family roots were in the Whitechurch and Tibradden area and, although she converted to Catholicism in her thirties, she requested that she be buried in Whitechurch churchyard in a family grave. At the time of her death she lived at Richmond Hill in Rathmines.

DUBLIN TOURISM

ANNIE SMITHSON
1873 - 1948

NOVELIST

LIVED
IN THIS HOUSE

...THAT ANNIE SMITHSON IS BURIED IN THE
GRAVEYARD IN WHITECHURCH

?

Ba bhanaltra cheantair i Ráth Fearnáin í Annie Smithson ar feadh na blianta fada agus bhí sí ar an úrscéalaí rómánsach ba mhó cáil a linne. Scríobh sí naoi gcinn déag d'úrscéalta ar a n-áirítear ceann darb ainm "The Weldons of Tibradden". Ba náisiúnach díograiseach í le linn Chogadh na Saoirse agus níos deireanaí fós bhí sí ina rúnaí ar Cheardchumann Altraí na hÉireann. Ba i gceantar an Teampaill Ghil agus Thigh Bródáin a bhí a préamhacha teaghlaigh agus fiú má d'iompair sí ar an gCaitleachas ina triocaidí de bhlianta, d'iarr sí go n-adhlacfaí i reilig an Teampaill Ghil í in uaigh an teaghlaigh. Tráth a bháis bhí sí ina cónaí i gCnoc Richmond i Ráth Maonais.

The Weldons of Tibradden

Annie M. P. Smithson

The Weldons of Tibradden follows the fortunes of three generations of the Weldon family beginning in the 1870s and ending in 1935. It is a fascinating story of success, courage, love and betrayal.

DUBLIN TOURISM

ANNIE SMITHSON
1873-1948

NOVELIST

LIVED
IN THIS HOUSE

...GO RAIBH ANNIE SMITHSON ADHLACTHA I REILIG
EAGLAIS NA HÉIREANN SA TEAMPALL GEAL

?

Major Henry Sirr became the town Major of Dublin in the late 18th century. He was in charge of Dublin's police and is probably best known for arresting Lord Edward Fitzgerald in 1798 and Robert Emmet in 1803. He had to have a military guard as protection against reprisals following these infamous arrests. Major Sirr's country residence was this house in Sandyford.

The illustration shown here, by George Cruikshank, depicts the arrest of Lord Edward by Major Sirr. It is one of life's ironies that both Lord Edward and Major Sirr are buried in St Werburgh's church.

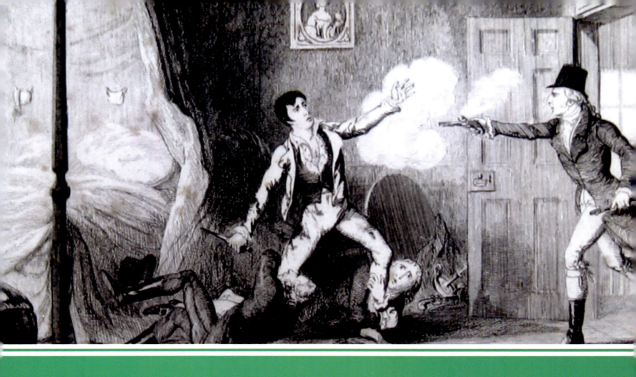

...THAT THE MOST FAMOUS REPUTED OCCUPANT OF SANDYFORD HOUSE, IN SANDYFORD VILLAGE, WAS MAJOR HENRY SIRR

MORAVIAN CEMETERY WHITECHURCH

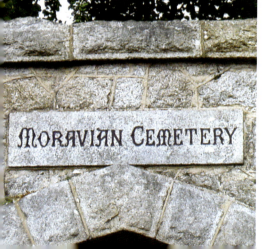

After 1620 Moravian Protestants were forced to choose between leaving their country or practising their beliefs secretly. This resulted in a general dispersion over northern Europe. In the early 18th century they initiated the first large-scale Protestant missionary movement. The Moravians emphasised simplicity of lifestyle and generosity with wealth.

In 1750 they arrived in Ireland and subsequently set up 40 preaching places and 18 churches. The Dublin church was in Bishop Street. Andrew Moller, a wealthy adherent, bequeathed land in Whitechurch for their cemetery. In the cemetery, the males were buried on one side, the females on the other.

did you know...

?

THE SEA

Robert Mallet, born in Dublin in 1810, is regarded as the father of seismology. He studied mathematics and science in Trinity College, Dublin and followed a career as a civil engineer and scientist. He first worked in his father's iron foundry in Capel Street. This was one of the best known foundries in Dublin. They made the iron railings around Trinity College and the original cast iron tower at Fastnet lighthouse. Among his many scientific interests was the study of earthquakes, and it is for this that he is best remembered.

A paper presented by Mallet to the Royal Irish Academy in 1846, on earthquake dynamics, is regarded as the foundation of modern seismology. Mallet is credited with being the first to use the words seismology and epicentre.

In November 1849, at Killiney beach, Mallet detonated kegs of gunpowder that he buried under the beach and measured the travel times of the shock waves. He also carried out tests on Dalkey Island the following year. These experiments at Killiney and Dalkey were the first such experiment in the world and were landmarks in the history of the study of earthquakes.

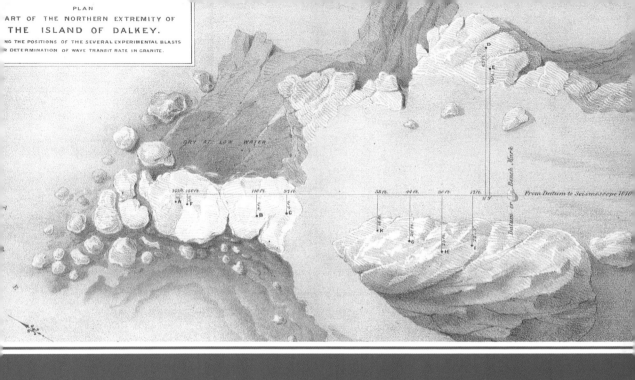

...THAT THE WORLD'S FIRST EXPERIMENTS IN SEISMOLOGY WERE CARRIED OUT ON KILLINEY BEACH AND DALKEY ISLAND

WILLIAMSTOWN MARTELLO TOWER

The Martello towers of Dublin are iconic buildings that were built along the coastline between 1804 and 1806. All the towers may look more or less the same, but some have unique features.

The tower at Booterstown was built in the inter tidal area and was literally in the sea at high tides. Most people see this tower from the DART railway line. This railway line effectively cut the tower off from the sea. However, for many years water was allowed into this area creating a lagoon around the tower. In the 20th century this water supply was cut off and the area around the tower was in filled. Today the ground floor of the tower is not visible as it is actually underground.

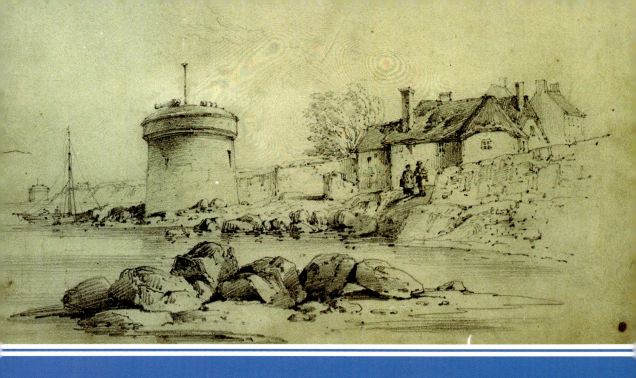

...THAT THE WILLIAMSTOWN MARTELLO TOWER IN BOOTERSTOWN USED TO BE IN THE SEA, AND WAS ALSO ONE STOREY HIGHER THAN IT APPEARS TODAY

?

STAINED-GLASS WINDOWS, ALL SAINTS' CHURCH

The two stained-glass windows are the work of Wilhelmina Geddes (1887-1955). She was born in County Leitrim and raised in Belfast. She became a member of An Tur Gloine (The Tower of Glass). On her death the Irish Times described her as "the finest stain glass artist of our time". These memorial windows, dating from 1920, show Michael with his spear and an orb, and Raphael with his staff and a jar of ointment. Unfortunately, a third window depicting the Archangel Gabriel was completely destroyed by fire in the 1920s.

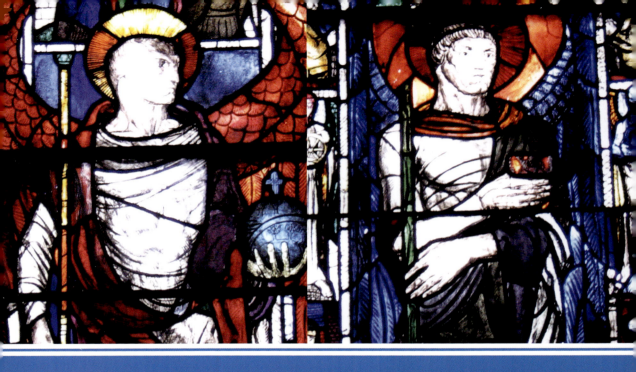

...THAT THESE DRAMATIC DEPICTIONS OF THE ARCHANGELS MICHAEL AND RAPHAEL CAN BE SEEN IN ALL SAINTS' CHURCH, CARYSFORT AVENUE, BLACKROCK

?

COLIEMORE HARBOUR DALKEY

In the 14th century the mouth of the River Liffey became heavily silted up which made the passage of ships dangerous. Dalkey became a convenient alternative for ships. They would anchor in Dalkey Sound and offload their goods. For many years Dalkey was the main landing area for Dublin although it is not believed that there was a harbour as such – the construction of the present harbour at Coliemore began in 1868. As a result of all this activity and trade, the village of Dalkey became very prosperous and it was during this time that the famous seven castles of Dalkey were built. But it was not only goods that passed through the port of Dalkey. A number of important people arrived and departed from it. These included the Lord Deputy, Philip de Courtney (1385), Sir John Talbot, later Earl of Shrewsbury (1414), Sir Anthony St Leger (1553) and the Viceroy, Sir John Perrot (1584).

...THAT DALKEY WAS ONCE DUBLIN'S MAIN PORT

?

GLASTHULE WORLD WAR II BOMBING

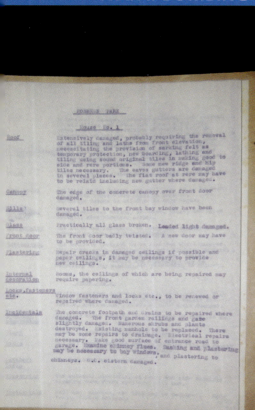

The customary peace and quiet of this sleepy part of Dublin was rudely disturbed on the evening of 20 December 1940 when Glasthule was the site of an attack by the German Luftwaffe. At around 7 pm an aircraft approached from the south-east, flying over Dalkey, and was heard diving to a height of just a few hundred feet.

A target indicator flare preceded the dropping of two bombs which injured three people. It was one of seven attacks on neutral Ireland during World War II. The bombs fell in the area around Rosmeen Gardens, Rosmeen Park, Martello Avenue and the train station. A report into the bomb damage was carried out by the Dún Laoghaire Burough Corporation, a page of which is shown here.

...THAT THE GERMAN LUFTWAFFE BOMBED
GLASTHULE DURING WORLD WAR II

?

JOHN MCCURDY

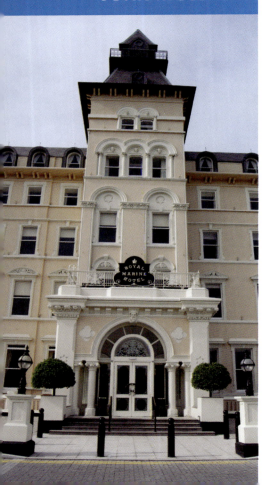

John McCurdy was an eminent 19th century architect and was the first president of the Royal Institute of Architects of Ireland. He lived in Elsinore in Dalkey. McCurdy worked on some of Dublin's best known buildings. He remodelled the Shelbourne Hotel, made additions to Monkstown Church and designed the building that houses TCD's Departments of Zoology and Physiology. But perhaps McCurdy's most unusual work was the East Wing of Kilmainham Gaol, built in the early 1860s. One of his next works was the Royal Marine Hotel in Dún Laoghaire. You could say he went from one form of accommodation to another!

...THAT THE PERSON WHO ORIGINALLY DESIGNED
THE ROYAL MARINE HOTEL IN DÚN LAOGHAIRE ALSO
DESIGNED THE EAST WING OF KILMAINHAM GAOL

?

George's Street was named in honour of King George IV who visited the town in 1821. In 1902 at a meeting of the Kingstown Urban District Council, it was proposed to rename George's Street O'Growney Street after a Father O'Growney who was involved in the Gaelic Revival. In 1920 Moran Street was proposed in honour of Patrick Moran, executed during the War of Independence in Mountjoy Prison (shown in the top picture on the far left the day before his execution). Moran had lived and worked in Blackrock and Dún Laoghaire. This renaming attempt failed narrowly. In 1966 it was proposed to rename the street Casement Street after Sandycove born Roger Casement (bottom left). It was the 50th anniversary of Casement's execution. In 1979 another proposal to rename the street Pearse Street was defeated. So, despite the other changes to the street over the years, the name has remained stubbornly the same. (For full details of proposed changes see Dún Laoghaire Borough Historical Society Journal No. 11, 2002).

...THAT THERE HAVE BEEN A NUMBER OF ATTEMPTS TO CHANGE THE NAME OF GEORGE'S STREET IN DÚN LAOGHAIRE

?

KILLINEY BEACH

Most of the stones that are on the beach at Killiney come from the glacial cliffs behind the beach. These stones were scoured by glaciers thousands of years ago and deposited in the Killiney area. There is spotted Ordovician volcanic rock called porphyry, from Lambay Island. There is also flint, a pale, white to brown coloured glassy rock that was scoured up from the base of the Irish sea.

The furthest travelled stones on the beach are the distinctive microgranite from Ailsa Craig, an island off the Ayrshire coast of Scotland. These distinctive stones, were brought by the Irish Sea glacier some 30,000 years ago. This microgranite from the Ailsa Craig (bottom left) is very popular for use as curling stones in the winter sport of curling.

...THAT THERE ARE BITS OF SCOTLAND ON
KILLINEY BEACH

?

In Greek legend he was the creator of the labyrinth on the island of Crete where King Minos imprisoned the Minotaur, a fearful creature who was half – man and half – bull.

This statue appropriately overlooks Ballinclea Park where a maze has been constructed.

Another statue inspired by literature is that of the Fiddler of Dooney in Stillorgan Shopping Centre. He was made famous by WB Yeats in his poem of the same name.

These two men in deep conversation in Sandyford village do not appear to have any literary history, but one would love to eavesdrop on their conversation.

...THAT THIS STATUE IN KILLINEY HILL PARK
IS OF DAEDALUS

?

The largest single quarry in the county was in Dalkey. This supplied stone for the construction of the harbour at Dún Laoghaire. The area around Barnacullia has also been extremely important, and provided stone for many of Dublin's buildings and footpaths.

However, not many people are aware that the coastal area provided a huge amount of building stone over the centuries. Today there is evidence of quarrying in a number of areas along the coast, including the Maretimo headland, Salthill, Bullock and Seapoint. At Sandycove a large amount of stone was removed in the past. This was probably quarried for the stone used in the construction of the Martello tower and Gun Battery in the early 19th century. In the photographs note the steep quarry walls and flat quarry floor below the Martello tower. Also note the boreholes on the boulder signifying quarry activity.

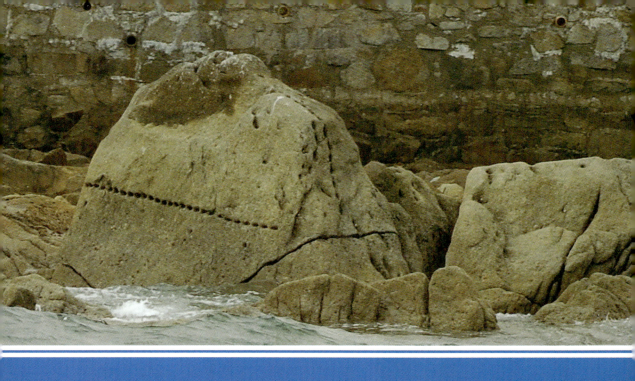

...THAT THE COAST OF DÚN LAOGHAIRE-RATHDOWN HAS BEEN THE LOCATION OF SIGNIFICANT QUARRY ACTIVITY IN THE PAST

?

"The Metals", as the path is known, runs for most of its length from Dún Laoghaire to Dalkey along the current railway line. At Dalkey it deviates from the railway line and goes uphill to the quarry. This path was originally a cart path along which carts laden with stone travelled to the harbour works at Dún Laoghaire, largely under the force of gravity. When the full cart travelled down, it pulled an empty cart from the harbour works back up the hill to Dalkey which was then filled for its return trip down the hill. Most of the original path of the Metals exists today although at one point in Dalkey it disappears into a small housing estate.

A walk along the Metals not only brings you back in time, but also brings you from one of the county's most scenic areas to another.

...THAT A PATH GOING FROM DÚN LAOGHAIRE TO DALKEY WAS ORIGINALLY MADE TO TRANSPORT STONE FROM THE QUARRY AT DALKEY FOR THE CONSTRUCTION OF THE HARBOUR AT DÚN LAOGHAIRE

?

'The Metals' a thugtar ar an gconair agus ar feadh an chuid is mó dá fad ó Dhún Laoghaire go Deilginis gabhann sé le hais an iarnróid atá ann faoi láthair. Ag Deilginis téann sé do leataobh ón iarnróid agus suas cnoc go dtí an cairéal ag Deilginis. Conair chairte a bhí sa chonair i dtús ama a mbíodh cairteacha ag taisteal uirthi faoi ualaigh chloch go dtí oibreacha Dhún Laoghaire le fórsa imtharraingthe. Tar éis don chairt teacht anuas lena hualach tharraing sí cairt fholamh ó oibreacha an chalafoirt ar ais suas an cnoc go Deilginis, áit a líonadh í le haghaidh an aistear fillte le fána.

Tá an chuid is mó de chonair bhunaidh na Metals fós ann inniu cé go n-imíonn sí ag pointe amháin i nDeilginis isteach in eastát beag tithíochta. Ní hamháin gur aistear siar san am a caitheadh atá sa tsiúlóid ar feadh na Metals, ach is aistear freisin é ó cheann go chéile de na ceantair is áille sa chontae.

...GO RAIBH CONAIR AG DUL Ó DHÚN LAOGHAIRE GO
DTÍ DEILGINIS A RINNEADH AN CHÉAD LÁ RIAMH CHUN
CLOCHA A AISTRIÚ ÓN GCAIRÉAL AG DEILGINIS GO DÚN
LAOGHAIRE CHUN AN CALAFORT A THÓGÁIL

?

KILLINEY LEAD MINE

Near the White Rock bathing place in Killiney is the abandoned entrance to an old lead mine. Like the larger mines at Ballycorus this lead mine was located at the junction between granite rock, formed by the slow cooling of magma, and Ordovician schists. The mine extended underneath the hill to a total length of some 350 metres. The mine had a long history and is first recorded in 1751. It appears on John Rocque's map of 1756. The mine was known as Mount Mapas Mine.

The mine was first closed in the late 18th century, but it reopened in 1825. During the later years of the works the lead mined at Killiney was transported by barge to Liverpool and was used in the manufacture of paint.

In Flann O'Brien's novel "The Dalkey Archive" the main character De Selby lives in Dalkey and claims to have mastered time with a substance called "DMP". With it he is able to create conditions in which he can converse with such figures as St John the Baptist in a cave near White Rock. Is this famous literary cave the old lead mine?

...THAT THERE WAS A LEAD MINE UNDER KILLINEY HILL

?

EAST PIER CANNON

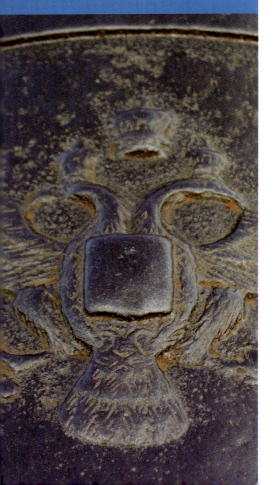

The cannon at the East Pier gardens in Dún Laoghaire is a familiar landmark, part of the spoils of the Crimean War, and an object for children to clamber over and fire at imaginary pirate ships in Scotsman's Bay. According to the Kingstown Town Commissioners minutes of 17 July 1857, £16 was raised from the townships rates for the purchase of one "Russian gun" from the Secretary for War, Lord Panmure. The 24lbs gun arrived and was placed on a carriage that had been made at the Royal Arsenal in Woolwich, London. The gun was originally on display at a platform along Queen's Road, near to the site of Dun Laoghaire Baths. When the road was widened, the cannon went into storage for 40 years and in 1974 it was put back on display at its present location at the East Pier gardens.

The Russian gun was one of nearly 3,000 that were captured during the Crimean War. Most of them were reportedly from the siege of Sebastopol – due to public discontent with the management of the war it is suspected that these numbers were exaggerated in order to show why the siege took so long. In the Treaty of Paris, which ended the war, it was agreed that each of the victors would receive cannons from the Russians, as trophies of their victory. Some of these Russian guns were put on display in towns throughout Britain and Ireland. In Ireland over 20 towns are believed to have applied for and received a Russian gun for display. You can see the double eagle and crown of the Romanov family crest on the Dún Laoghaire cannon today.

...THAT THE GUN AT THE EAST PIER GARDENS IS A
TROPHY FROM THE CRIMEAN WAR

?

AN GUNNA MÓR AG AN BPIARA THOIR

Is críochchomhartha aitheanta an gunna mór ag an bPiara Thoir agus cuid d'éadálacha an Chogaidh Chrimé; is rud é a bhíonn na páistí ag dreapadh agus ag ligean orthu go bhfuil siad ag scaoileadh urchair le longa foghlaí mara i gCuan na nAlbanach. De réir mhiontuairiscí Coimisinéirí Bhaile Kingstown, an 17 Iúil, 1857, bailíodh 16 punt ó rátaí na mbailecheantar chun aon 'Russian gun' a cheannach ón Rúnaí Cogaidh, an Tiarna Panmure. Tháinig an gunna 24 phunt agus cuireadh ar charráiste é a tógadh san Armlann Ríoga i Woolwich, Londain. Bhí an gunna ar taispeáint ar dtús ar sheastán ar bhóthar na Banríona, gar do na Folcthaí. Nuair a fairsingíodh an bóthar cuireadh an gunna mór i stóras ar feadh 40 bliain agus i 1974 cuireadh ar ais ar taispeáint é san áit a bhfuil sé faoi láthair ag gairdíní an Phiara Thoir.

Ba cheann é an gunna Rúiseach de nach mór 3,000 gunna a gabhadh i gcaitheamh an Chogaidh Chríme. Bhain a bhformhór díobh le léigear Sebastopol de réir tuairiscí - táthar amhrasach faoi go ndearnadh áiféis maidir lena líon chun a léiriú do phobal a bhí míshásta le bainistíocht an chogaidh cén fáth gur mhair an léigear chomh fada agus a mhair. Comhaontaíodh i gConradh Phárais a chuir deireadh leis an gcogadh sin go bhfaigheadh gach ceann de na buaiteoirí gunnaí móra ó na Rúisigh mar thrófaithe an bhua. Cuireadh cuid de na gunnaí Rúiseacha seo ar taispeáint i mbailte ar fud na Breataine Móire agus na hÉireann. Meastar gur iarraidh agus go bhfuair breis is 20 baile in Éirinn gunna Rúiseach lena chur ar taispeáint. Tá iolar décheannach agus coróin chírín an teaghlaigh Romanov le feiceáil ar an ngunna mór sa lá atá inniu ann.

...GUR TRÓFAÍ ÓAN GCÉAD CHOGADH DOMHANDA ATÁ
SA GHUNNA AG GAIRDÍNÍ AN PHIARA THOIR

?

TERNS ON DALKEY ISLAND

There are five species of tern breeding in Ireland, three of which breed in Dalkey. They resemble a small gull, but with a black cap and distinctly forked tail. This feature has earned them the name "sea swallow". Terns hover and dive to catch small fish such as sandeels and sprats. They arrive on our shores in May and depart in late summer. Most spend the winter along the west coast of Africa, although the Arctic Tern continues to the southern oceans surrounding Antarctica – a mighty journey!

The Roseate Tern is a threatened species in Europe, and has been the main focus of the conservation efforts on the Dalkey islands. This species will only breed among colonies of other tern species, and prefers to nest under cover: unlike our other terns, they will readily use man-made nest boxes, and can be seen in the Dalkey colony between May and August. In late summer as many as one hundred Roseate Terns may roost each evening on Maiden Rock, making this one of the best places in Europe for birdwatchers to see this enigmatic species. Most of these roosting birds come from Europe's largest colony on Rockabill Island, off the north Dublin coast, and they gather in Dalkey and south Dublin Bay before beginning their migration to Africa.

...THAT DALKEY ISLAND IS ONE OF THE BEST PLACES TO VIEW TERNS

?

The Martello tower in Sandycove is the famous setting for the first chapter of "Ulysses" where "Stately, plump Buck Mulligan came from the stairhead, bearing a bowl of lather on which a mirror and a razor lay crossed. A yellow dressinggown, ungirdled, was sustained gently behind him on the mild morning air".

A key landmark in Dún Laoghaire-Rathdown features in one famous exchange in "Ulysses":
"Tell me now", Stephen said, "poking the boy's shoulder with the book, what is a pier."
"A pier, sir," Armstrong said. "A thing out in the water. A kind of bridge. Kingstown pier, sir."
Some laughed again: mirthless but with meaning. Two in the back bench whispered. Yes. They knew: had never learned nor ever been innocent. All. With envy they watched their faces: Edith, Ethel, Gerty, Lily. Their likes: their breaths, too, sweetened with tea and jam, their bracelets tittering in the struggle.
"Kingstown pier," Stephen said. "Yes, a disappointed bridge." The words troubled their gaze.

However, not many people are aware that the second chapter is set in Summerfield House, Dalkey. Now a private house it was once the Clifton School. Like every chapter of "Ulysses" there is a theme and in this chapter it is history. Stephen Dedalus is giving a history lesson to his pupils (Joyce once taught at this school) although neither is paying too much attention.

...THAT CHAPTER TWO OF JAMES JOYCE'S ULYSSES IS SET
IN DÚN LAOGHAIRE-RATHDOWN

?

If you cross the railway line at Blackrock and walk a little north you will find a very unusual rock formation on the seashore. If you look closely at the stone you can see that this rock seems to have been broken up and cemented together again. It is a great example of the powerful geological forces at play.

Around 400 million years ago the granite in the area slowly cooled – this took about 20 million years. When it had nearly cooled completely, a build-up of gas exploded through the rock. Once the gas had escaped, molten granite filled the cracks and bonded the angular rocks together. This formation is called an "explosion breccia".

On a similar geological note, Blackrock is so called because it is here that dark limestone contrasts with the lighter-coloured granite found along the coast south of here. The fault between the granite and the carboniferous limestone is located at the northern end of the pond in Blackrock Park.

...THAT THERE IS A RARE ROCK FORMATION
AT BLACKROCK

?

First used for climbing in the early 1940s, its rock faces have been used by generations of Irish climbers in learning and honing their skills. To date there are some 350 recognised climbs in the quarry. They range from "Difficult" to "Extreme". More people climb here each year than in the rest of Ireland. Joss Lynam, the doyen of Irish climbers who made his first ascent in Dalkey in 1948, was seen as recently as 2006 abseiling down Winder's Slab to celebrate his 82nd birthday.

But it is not just the experts who climb at Dalkey. The quarry has routes to suit almost all abilities and is where many people have been first introduced to the sport.

...THAT DALKEY QUARRY IS THE CRADLE OF IRISH ROCK CLIMBING

?

Chuathas ag dreapadóireacht inti den chéad uair i luathbhlianta na 1940aidí agus ó shin i leith bhaineadh na glúine de dhreapadóirí Éireannacha áis as éadain na carraige inti le scileanna a fhoghlaim agus a thabhairt chun foirfeachta. Go dáta tá thart ar 350 bealach dreapadóireachta sa chairéal atá aitheanta (agus a bhfuil cur síos déanta orthu); bealaí de gach uile ghrád atá iontu ó Dheacair go thar bheith Deacair. Bíonn níos mó daoine ag dreapadóireacht anseo gach bliain ná mar bhíonn in Éirinn uile. Chonacthas Joss Lynam an fear ab fhaide atá a ainm in airde i measc dhreapadóirí na hÉireann agus a dhreap éadan carraige den chéad uair i nDeilginis i 1948 chomh deireanach le 2006 ag téadtuirlingt síos Leac Winder chun lá a bhreithe tá 82 bhliain ó shin a cheiliúradh.

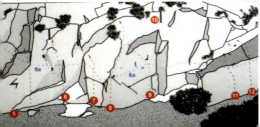

...GURBH I GCAIRÉAL DEILGINIS BA THÚISCE A CHUAIGH ÉIREANNAIGH I MBUN DREAPADÓIREACHTA AR CHARRAIGEACHA MAR SPÓRT.

ATMOSPHERIC RAILWAY

In the early years of the railway era there was a great debate between the merits of locomotive and atmospheric railways. The first line in the world to be laid on the atmospheric system was laid between Dún Laoghaire and Dalkey in 1844. It was nearly 3kms long. The train ran along rails, but instead of being propelled by an engine it was propelled along an iron tube 15 inches in diameter, which acted as a suction pipe. A pump moved air through the tube at the top of which was a slit through which an arm extended to the carriage. The problem of keeping the tube airtight (which was essential) was very difficult and was not assisted by rats eating at the tube's leather seals. This resulted in the closure of the world's first atmospheric railway in 1854. It also survived long enough to be the last one in existence in Britain and Ireland. However, a remnant of the original line still exists – a bridge on Castle Park Road now covers a redundant part of the famous Atmospheric Railway.

...THAT DÚN LAOGHAIRE AND DALKEY WERE THE FIRST PLACES TO HAVE AN ATMOSPHERIC RAILWAY

?

The shoreline between Killiney and Bray used to extend up to two kilometres out into today's sea. The land was gradually eroded and submerged under the Irish Sea. In the shallow waters near Corke Abbey lies a 6,200-year-old forest of collapsed Scotch pine trees protruding from the shifting sands, part of a now-buried river valley. Above and around it lies a submerged railway line extending from Bray harbour to Shanganagh, and fragments of submerged fisherman's cottages, coastal protection works, landing places and the old military road. There are also shipwrecks such as the Lady Harriett (1852), the Endeavour (1861), the Pensiero (1873), the Mary Celine (1926), the Erne (1936) and the Leonie which, on the 30 September 1876, came ashore beside a now-lost Martello tower. And still the sea does not give up all it's secrets.

...THAT IN ADDITION TO SHIPWRECKS THAT LIE BENEATH THE SURF, SEA AND SAND OF KILLINEY BAY THERE ARE ALSO BUILDINGS AND A SUBMERGED LANDSCAPE

NEAR THIS SPOT DURING THE STORM OF
XMAS EVE 1895 THE CREW OF ONE OF THE
KINGSTOWN LIFE BOATS EMBARKED ON THEIR
LAST MISSION OF MERCY IN AN ATTEMPT TO REACH
A WRECK THE BOAT WAS CAPSIZED AND ALL HER
GALLANT CREW WERE DROWNED
THEIR NAMES ARE HERE SUBSCRIBED

ALEX^R WILLIAMS^{COX} HENRY WILLIAMS$^{EX.COX}$
FRANCIS SAUNDERS GEORGE SAUNDERS
EDWARD SHANNON PATRICK POWER
EDWARD CROWE   JOHN BAKER
HENRY UNDERHILL JOHN BARTLEY
WILLIAM DUNPHY   THOMAS DUNPHY
EDWARD MURPHY   FRANCIS M^C DONALD
JAMES RYAN

On 24 December 1895 the No. 2 Lifeboat at Dún Laoghaire capsized while proceeding to the assistance of the SS Palme of Finland. The Palme was en route from Liverpool to South America when it was hit by a storm and sought shelter in Dún Laoghaire. However, high winds and heavy seas dragged it to Monkstown. The Dún Laoghaire Lifeboat was launched from near the East Pier to rescue the crew of the Palme. Crowds watched from the shore as the lifeboat capsized about 600 metres from the Palme. All 15 lifeboat men were drowned. Each Christmas Eve a ceremony is held by the RNLI at sea outside the harbour to commemorate what is the largest single lifeboat disaster in the history of the Irish service.

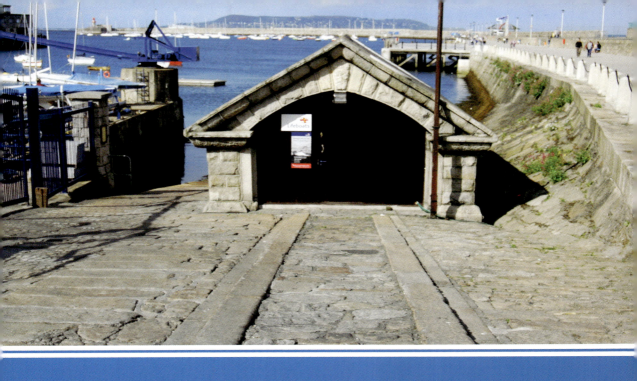

...THAT ON CHRISTMAS EVE EVERY YEAR MEMBERS OF THE ROYAL NATIONAL LIFEBOAT INSTITUTE PUT A WREATH INTO THE WATERS OUTSIDE DÚN LAOGHAIRE HARBOUR TO COMMEMORATE AN 1895 LIFEBOAT DISASTER

Most people view south Dublin Bay from a distance – from the Rock Road, from the piers, from the DART. It is a beautiful expanse of water. But it is much more than that. Dublin Bay helps to support thousands of birds and as such it is a designated Special Protection Area. The Bay is also a Special Area of Conservation. Its extensive areas of sand and mudflats are protected habitats under the European Union Habitats Directive. The birds that frequent the area include Oystercatcher, Ringed Plover, Sanderling, Dunlin, Redshank, Snipe, Little Egret, Cormorant, Bar Tailed Godwit, Curlew, Purple Sandpiper (below left), Tern - including the extremely rare Roseate Tern - and various types of gull. Notable annual visitors to the Bay are Brent Geese (above left) which occur in numbers of international importance (they come from Canada every year). One of the great hazards to these birds is people walking their dogs when the tide is out.

...THAT DUBLIN BAY, RIGHT UP TO DÚN LAOGHAIRE'S WEST PIER, IS AN INTERNATIONALLY - IMPORTANT SITE FOR WILDLIFE

?

There were once 28 Martello towers and associated gun batteries along the Dublin coastline from Bray to Balbriggan. The tower in the People's Park was tower number 12. The towers were built by the British in the early 19th century to defend the area against a feared invasion by the French. Just 21 of these towers and their batteries exist today. The tower in Glasthule was demolished around 1849.

The British had built the towers to this particular design after their bitter experience of attacking one at Cape Martella in Corsica which had provided staunch defence against their attack in 1794.

According to one British admiral, "The Fortitude and Juno were ordered against [the tower], without making the least impression by a continued cannonade of two hours and a half; and the former ship being very much damaged by red-hot shot, both hauled off...The number of men in the Tower were 33; only two were wounded".

...THAT THERE USED TO BE A MARTELLO TOWER IN
THE PEOPLE'S PARK IN GLASTHULE

?

If you walked the length of Library Road in Dún Laoghaire you would do very well to spot an unusual looking building at the end of a footpath beside a children's playground. This red structure gives little indication of what lies within.

In fact the red structure is merely a casing for an oratory built on the grounds of what was then the Dominican Convent in 1919. Sister Concepta Lynch painstakingly decorated this tiny oratory, measuring roughly four metres by three metres, in the 1920s and 1930s. She spent her evenings decorating the chapel with beautiful Celtic inspired designs in wonderfully vibrant colours. The oratory is regarded as a masterpiece of Celtic revival art. It also features stained-glass windows from the Harry Clarke Studio.

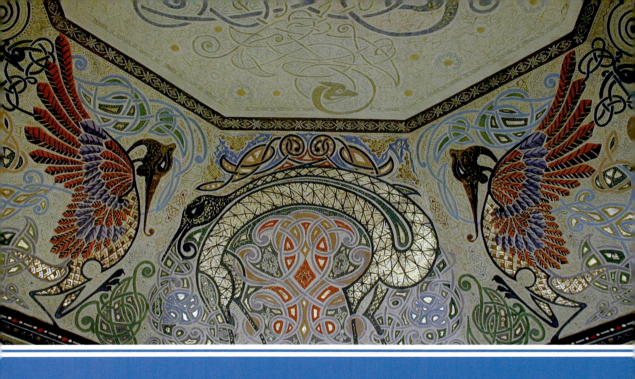

...THAT THERE IS A HIDDEN GEM OF CELTIC REVIVAL ART IN DÚN LAOGHAIRE

?

MORAN PARK HOUSE

Now called Moran Park House, the Harbour Master's House was built in the 1830s. Before this the harbour master, Lieutenant William Hutchison from Kildare, was attached to the Ballast Board and he lived at Bullock Harbour. However, owing to the increase in the number of ships using the harbour at Dún Laoghaire (then Kingstown) £800 was provided for the construction of the house. Hutchison was its first resident.

Hutchison was in charge of the harbour until 1874. In recognition for bravery when going to the rescue of the brig "Ellen" in 1821 and the "Duke" 1829, both of which were wrecked on Sandycove point, he received an engraved silver teapot. In 1829 he received the RNLI "Gold Medal" for bravery. He was awarded the silver medal for exceptional bravery when attempting to rescue Capt Boyd during the disastrous storm of 8 February 1861. In recognition of the first harbour master, in 1989 the Harbour Company named its first official vessel after Hutchison.

...THAT THE DÚN LAOGHAIRE HARBOUR MASTER HAD
HIS OWN RESIDENCE

?

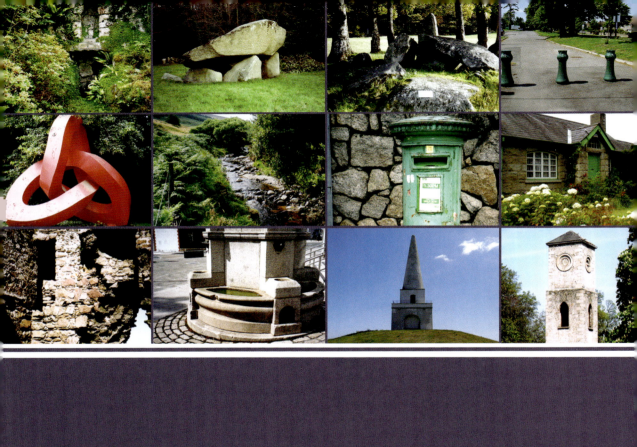

did you know...

GENERAL

?

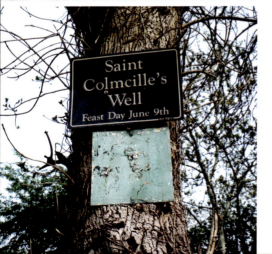

Holy wells are distributed widely throughout the country. There are numerous ones in Dún Laoghaire-Rathdown. Many of these are on private lands. In fact there are a number in back gardens. Among those with public accesss are two in Stepaside, one dedicated to St Patrick and one to St James.

St Patrick's Well was visited annually on 17 March, as recently as 20 years ago and is well cared for. It is on private grounds. St James' Well lies in a laneway in the public golf course. St James' Day is 1 May.

Another well in south Dublin is St Colmcille's Well near Orlagh College. It is easily accessed and well labelled. The water is drunk and is also applied to sore ears. The feast of St Colmcille is on 9 June.

...THAT HOLY WELLS HAVE BEEN VENERATED IN IRELAND
FOR THOUSANDS OF YEARS, LONG BEFORE THE COMING
OF CHRISTIANITY

?

PORTAL DOLMENS

A dolmen is our oldest megalithic monument and dates from around 2,500 BC. Portal dolmens have two upright stones of similar height which support the capstone in front making a type of portal or entrance to the tomb chamber. A varying number of stones support the back.

There are seven dolmens in this area. The three illustrated here, Brennanstown, Ballybrack and Kilternan, have their capstones still in place. All of them except Ballybrack are on private land.

All the portal tombs would have been originally covered with earth and stones to form a mound.

...THAT THE AREA LYING BETWEEN THE THREE ROCK
MOUNTAIN AND THE SEA IS PARTICULARLY RICH
IN ITS NUMBER OF DOLMENS

COLLAPSED PORTAL DOLMENS

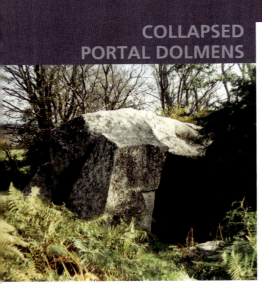

It is believed in the case of the Mount Venus dolmen that the capstone may have been displaced by an earthquake. There are no suggestions as to what happened to the other two.

Dolmens were originally covered over with earth and stones of which there are no remains today and therefore they can be described as skeleton structures or as degraded and denuded tombs.

All three of these dolmens are on private land.

...THAT THE LAST THREE OF OUR LOCAL DOLMENS –
LARCH HILL, MOUNT VENUS AND GLENSOUTHWELL –
ARE COLLAPSED WITH THEIR HEADSTONES FALLEN

?

In Dalkey one can still see tram tracks in the old tram yard on the main street while at the People's Park Dún Laoghaire, Monkstown Avenue and Dalkey Hill bases of the poles supporting the tram wires are today used as ornamental bollards.

The first trams in Dublin were drawn by horse and the service began in 1872. The first electric trams began to run in 1896. The service to Dalkey from Sackville Street had taken two hours by horse drawn tram but just 55 minutes by electric tram.

The fares for a single journey in 1937 was 5 pence (return was 8 pence). You could take your bicycle on the tram for 3 pence but there was an early park-and-ride facility in Dalkey where you could leave your bicycle for 2 pence a day.

The last tram ran from Dalkey on 10 July 1949. An era had ended but today, if you look, there are still reminders of this bygone age of public transport.

...THAT TODAY THERE ARE STILL PRESERVED REMINDERS
OF THE TRAM ERA

?

Ice houses were constructed in the grounds of large country houses, and served as the only reliable means of refrigeration in the 18th and early 19th centuries. An ice house usually consisted of a structure with a short passage leading to a much larger chamber with a shallow, domed roof, and an inverted cone base below ground, in which the ice was stored. It was stocked with layers of ice from local ponds or rivers.

...THAT ICE HOUSES WERE THE FORERUNNERS OF
THE REFRIGERATOR

?

RED SQUIRRELS

To date two populations of red squirrel in Ireland have become extinct. The first time was in the 1700s when forest clearance and hunting them for their fur wiped out the population. They were successfully reintroduced from England in the 1800s and spread rapidly. But now they are at risk again.

In 1911 there was a wedding in County Longford in Lord Granard's family home and a well-meaning guest brought a present of six pairs of grey squirrels from Canada. These were released into the wild and their numbers increased so enormously that the grey squirrel now lives in over half the country. Unfortunately, they carry a virus, harmless to them but fatal to the smaller red squirrel. An antidote is being sought.

In Dún Laoghaire-Rathdown, grey squirrels are numerous, inhabiting parks and gardens as they like broad-leaved trees. Reds can be seen on Killiney Hill, Carrickgollogan Wood and Ticknock Wood as they prefer conifers.

To aid population recovery, around 60 red squirrels are now in a breeding programme in Beleek Wood, Mayo where greys do not exist.

...THAT OUR RED SQUIRRELS ARE UNDER THREAT FOR THE THIRD TIME IN THEIR HISTORY

Wild orchids mostly occur in unimproved grassland areas where nutrient levels are low and where management practices maintain a low, open sward.

Orchids can appear from as early as May, through to July and August. They may be seen in Kilternan, in Loughlinstown, on the steep, dry banks along the Bray Road, and in patches along the Vico Road overlooking the sea. Increased use of fertilisers, expansion of the road network, and inappropriate management of grassland areas, all contribute to the loss of these species from the county.

While orchid numbers are not high, the most frequently seen species in the county include (as shown above) the Common Spotted Orchid (Dactylorhiza fuchsii), Pyramidal Orchid (Anacamptis pyramidalis), Common Twayblade (Listera ovata), and the Bee Orchid (Ophrys apifera). The small but beautifully spiral-shaped Autumn Lady's-tresses (Spiranthes spiralis) is quite rare. Have you seen this one?

...THAT WILD ORCHIDS GROW IN DÚN LAOGHAIRE-RATHDOWN

?

In recent years many interesting sculptures have brightened our environment. Roadside designs should be striking but simple as motorists must be able to see them but not be distracted by having to study them.

The sculptures shown here may be found in the Sandyford Industrial Estate, at the roundabout at Leopardstown and at the junction of Whitechurch Road and College Road.

...THAT YOU DO NOT HAVE TO GO INTO A GALLERY
IN ORDER TO ENJOY MODERN ART

?

The Glencullen River (main picture), is a tributary of the Dargle and forms part of the county boundary with Wicklow.

The Loughlinstown River, shown here at Heronford bridge (top), has three tributaries which flow through Kilternan, Kilgobbin and Cabinteely.

The Little Dargle River (below) flows from Ticknock, through Marlay Park to Ballinteer. It is shown here at Broadford. It then disappears underground on its way to the river Dodder.

Other rivers include the Slang, the Owendoher and the Deansgrange Stream.

...THAT DÚN LAOGHAIRE - RATHDOWN HAS SEVERAL SMALL RIVERS WHOSE EXISTENCE AND BEAUTIES OFTEN GO UNNOTICED BY THE PUBLIC

?

Four trial letter boxes were set up in Jersey and were so successful they spread over Britain and reached Ireland in 1856. Since then there have been over 150 different designs but all boxes carried a distinctive marking. The original boxes were all green but were later painted an eye-catching red.

Up to 1922 in Ireland the boxes carried the royal cipher of the reigning monarch (a crown and the initials VR, GR or ER). Some pillar boxes had the letters intertwined in a monogram but wall boxes bore the letters in plain block capitals. Of the 4,675 boxes in use today, one fifth are still from this period.

After independence, Irish pillar boxes were painted green. Most boxes retained the royal cipher, but some had it removed. Traces of this alteration can sometimes be seen. One group of boxes did not need this attention. Manufactured between 1879 and 1887, the cipher appears to have been forgotten and the box just states "Post Office" like the one (above) in Sandyford.

Ireland then produced its own markings – the initials SE for Saorstat Eireann, a harp, the initials P&T and, since 1984, the An Post logo. Many new boxes are plain.

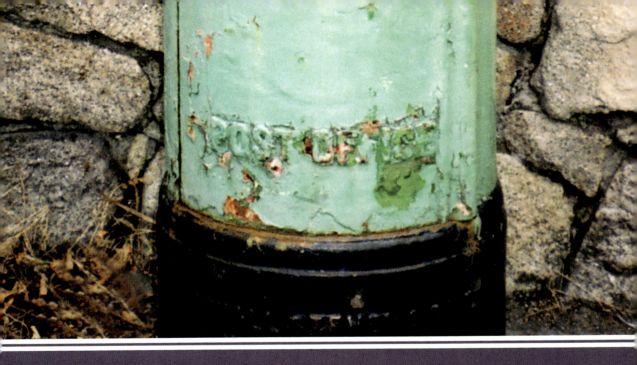

...THAT THE ROADSIDE PILLAR BOX WAS THE IDEA OF
THE NOVELIST ANTHONY TROLLOPE IN 1852

?

One of the measures taken to deal with the conditions that fostered such ill health was to provide better housing for the working class. Thus, the Labourers Act of 1906 stated that "comfortable, four-roomed cottages with from half to one acre should be available to all manual workers earning under 15 shillings weekly" at a very modest rent. The Local Government Board arranged a competition to find the most suitable designs, at a cost limit of £130. Some 400 submissions were received, two of which were erected for display (as illustrated left) at the 1907 Irish International Exhibition in Dublin.

The primary considerations for these cottages were a southward-facing aspect, suitable damp-proof materials, effective ventilation and drainage to a suitable outfall. Sash windows and half-doors were preferred, and fireplaces were to be provided in each room.

Few of the original cottages survive, but later versions on the same principles (both single and two-storey types) may be seen at various locations in Dún Laoghaire - Rathdown.

INTERIOR OF ARTIZAN'S COTTAGE (B).

...THAT A HUNDRED YEARS AGO 16 OUT OF EVERY 100 DEATHS IN IRELAND WERE DUE TO PULMONARY TUBERCULOSIS

?

About a thousand years ago, a papal edict declared that the symbol of a rooster be placed on top of every church to recall Peter's betrayal of Christ. It was logical that the rooster became incorporated in the weather-vane already on the church. However, weather-cocks are now rarely found on churches.

In the Middle Ages, as the nobility gained ascendancy, weather-vanes with heraldic motifs began to appear. Vanes with banners, pennants and flags were popular. Lesser ranks were allowed pennants with double tails which became the prototype for a style of weather-vane.

Later the weather-vane bore the symbol of the business of the house on which it was erected. This custom is still practiced, with a recent example of a horse at Leopardstown Racecourse.

...WHY MANY WEATHER-VANES ARE SHAPED LIKE
ROOSTERS AND CALLED WEATHER-COCKS

?

Ley lines are alignments of ancient sites stretching across a landscape. The existence of these straight lines is easy to see on a map, but the causes of these alignments are disputed.

Ley lines are believed, by some people, to show a special mystical or psychic energy which can be detected by dowsing. In the same way that a forked hazel twig or bent metal coat hangers can detect the presence of water, they can also pick up a magnetic field above a ley line. Ley lines were shown by Xavier Guichard to centre on a small village in eastern France. Please note that the lines on our local area map run in a direction which if elongated sufficiently may converge there!

Sceptics dismiss the existence of ley lines.

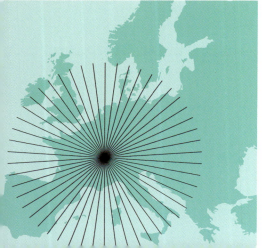

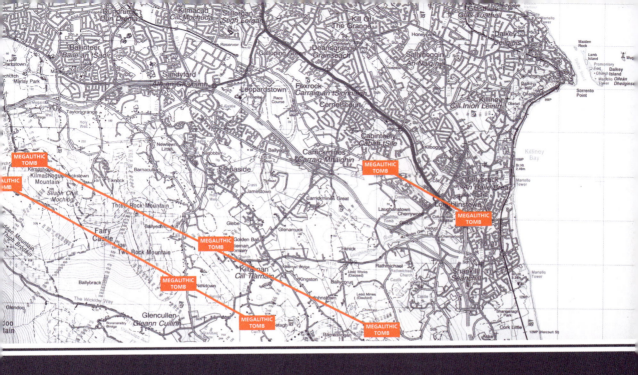

...WHAT A LEY LINE IS

?

HEN HOUSES

The doorway above was photographed in Stepaside, but similar examples can be found outside the Dún Laoghaire-Rathdown area. The second picture is from a farm in Westmeath.

Henhouses were built this way into a wall which was close to the farm house and as the wall was sufficiently thick, it gave enough room to enclose the hens for the night. The entrance would be blocked with a gate, thus providing protection from predators.

...THAT THIS CURIOUS-SHAPED DOORWAY IN A STONE WALL WAS REALLY THE ENTRANCE TO A HENHOUSE

?

THE RATHDOWN SLABS

There are 32 known Rathdown grave slabs in the Dublin area, of which the majority have been found in Dun Laoghaire-Rathdown. These distinct slabs were first written about in 1781. No two Rathdown slabs are alike, but they do have unique characteristics not found elsewhere in Ireland. They are made of granite and are around four or five inches thick.

Their decoration consists mainly of concentric circles, cup marks, herringbone patterns, semi-circular loops and some crosses. According to archaeologist Chris Corlett in 'The Antiquities of Old Rathdown', "frequently the decoration on the slabs does not fit readily within the traditional range of Christian symbols, but the meaning of any special symbolism has been lost over time". One theory is that the people who made the slabs were Vikings who had settled in this area and had become Christian and the design of the slabs fused their past religious symbols with Christian ones.

Rathdown slabs can be found in Rathmichael Old Church, Ballyman, Dalkey, Kilgobbin, Tully, Rathfarnham, Whitechurch and St Nahi's. The slabs pictured here are from Rathmichael and Kilgobbin.

...THAT THE GRAVE SLABS IN THESE PHOTOS ARE KNOWN AS THE RATHDOWN SLABS AS THEY ARE MOSTLY FOUND IN THIS AREA

?

GARDEROBE

This toilet was situated at the end of a short passage set inside the actual wall of a castle. It had a wooden or stone seat and waste fell down inside the wall to an opening at ground level outside the castle where it could be cleared away.

The odour in these garderobes was pungent. Because this deterred moths, the inhabitants of the castle kept their clothes in the short passage.

In other words the robes were guarded and the word "garderobe" is the forerunner of the modern word "wardrobe".

...THAT A MEDIEVAL TOILET WAS CALLED
A "GARDEROBE"

?

HORSE TROUGHS

At one time horse troughs were found on all main roads. They were often at a junction, or at the top of a hill, so that horses could drink and renew their energy.

The trough shown in the main picture is part of the Usher Memorial in Dundrum. It was ahead of its time and could perhaps be considered one of the first service stations because it also provided drinking water for the drivers. Water troughs can still be seen in Dundrum, Monkstown and Killiney.

...THAT HORSE TROUGHS COULD BE CONSIDERED THE FORERUNNERS OF PETROL STATIONS

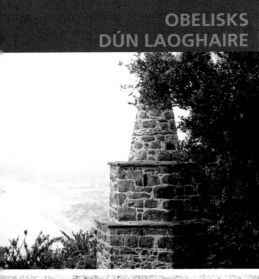

An obelisk is a tall tapering, usually four-sided, stone pillar with a pyramidal top. They were built as memorials, as landmarks, or to provide employment in hard times.

Killiney Obelisk and its small companion Mapas Tower were built in 1742 as famine relief works to help the poor after a particularly hard winter.

Stillorgan Obelisk was built in 1727 at the instigation of Lord Allen to provide local employment that year during the famine. This obelisk was designed by Edward Lovett Pearce who also designed the Irish Houses of Parliament (now the Bank of Ireland at College Green). It may also have been built as a memorial to Lady Allen, but she was not buried there.

...THAT THERE ARE SEVERAL OBELISKS IN THE DUN LAOGHAIRE REGION

?

In the days before watches, a clock mounted on the circular portion of the tower showed the time to all.

And for those workers who were out of sight of the clock as they were working in the fields, the large bell housed in the tower rang out for meals and for the end of the working day.

In fact the Latin word for a bell is "cloca" giving us our modern word "clock".

Killakee still has its bell and its rope in working order as can be seen in this view upwards through the tower.

...THAT THESE BELL TOWERS OVERLOOKING THE OLD FARM YARDS AT MARLAY PARK AND KILLAKEE WERE OF GREAT USE TO THE FARM WORKERS

?

PINEAPPLES

In the 17th century when colonial sea captains returned from their travels, they put a pineapple on their gate posts as a sign that they had returned and were ready to welcome their friends.

Later, the pineapple, a very expensive fruit, was the centre piece of a hostess's table and showed the lengths to which she had gone to ensure that her guests felt that every detail had been attended to for their pleasure.

Stone pineapples can still be seen on gateposts. There are wrought iron examples in Airfield, and small finials of pineapple design can even be found on screens surrounding coffee shops!! Check out your local!

...THAT THE PINEAPPLE HAS BEEN THE UNIVERSAL SYMBOL OF HOSPITALITY AND WELCOME FOR CENTURIES ALL OVER THE WORLD

A blacksmith works with elemental fire and magical iron and so was thought to have special powers. It was believed that he could heal the sick, and also that if a couple were married by a blacksmith their marriage would be happy.

Horseshoes are lucky because they are made of iron, a magical metal which can withstand fire. They were commonly held in place by seven nails. From ancient times seven was considered an important number. Life was divided into seven ages, there are seven deadly sins, seven days in a week, a seventh child has special powers, a rainbow has seven colours…

Nowadays things have changed. Modern horse shoes have eight nails and there are no working forges in our area – but we do still have reminders at Barnhill Road in Dalkey and in Cross Avenue in Dún Laoghaire, both shown on left.

...THAT A FORGE WAS ASSOCIATED WITH GOOD FORTUNE AS BLACKSMITHS AND HORSE SHOES WERE CONSIDERED TO BE LUCKY

Well, there does not appear to be one single answer. Some yew trees were actually there before a church was built as the priest often preached under a yew tree if the village could not afford a church.

In 1307 King Edward I ordered yew trees to be planted in churchyards to offer protection to the buildings.

Traditionally a church has only two yew trees, one on the gateway leading to the main door and the second on the path to the minor door.

Yews are poisonous so, by planting them in churchyards, cattle, which were not allowed to graze on hallowed land, were safe from eating yew. Yew was the traditional wood used for making longbows, and planting in churchyards ensured availability in times of need.

Yew branches, on touching the ground, take root and sprout again. This became the symbol of death, rebirth and therefore of immortality.

...WHY YEW TREES ARE PLANTED IN CHURCHYARDS

?

Ní léir go bhfuil aon fhreagra aonair ar an gceist. Bhí roinnt crann iúir ann iarbhír sular tógadh séipéal mar is minic gur faoi chrann iúir a thug an sagart seanmóir mura raibh sráidbhaile in acmhainn séipéal a thógáil.

I 1307 d'ordaigh an Rí Edward I crainn iúir a chur i gcealla chun na foirgnimh a chosaint. De réir traidisiúin ní bhíonn ag séipéal ach dhá chrann iúir, ceann amháin ag an ngeata a dtéann conair uaidh go dtí an príomhdhoras agus cheann eile ar an gconair go dtí an doras tánaiste.

Is crann nimhneach é an crann iúir agus de bhrí gur cuireadh i gcill é bhí cosaint ag beithígh ar an nimh a bhí ann a ithe toisc é bheith diúltaithe dóibhsin iníor ar thalamh beannaithe. Adhmad an iúir an mianach as a ndearnadh an bogha fada de réir traidisiúin agus dá gcuirtí iúr i gcill é bhíothas cinnte go mbeadh fáil ar an adhmad in am an ghátair.

A luaithe is a dhéanann craobh an iúir teagmháil leis an talamh cuireann sé fréamhacha agus eascraíonn crann nua astu sin. B'amhlaidh go ndearnadh siombail de den bhás, den athbhreith agus dá réir den tsíormharthain.

...AN FÁTH GO GCUIRTEAR CRAINN IÚIR I GCEALLA

?

In 1417 as a first attempt to brighten the streets, the Mayor of London asked for lanterns to be hung outside between Halloween and Candlemas. Three hundred years later these lanterns became required by law, and householders with a property on a street, lane or passage faced a fine of one shilling if they failed to show a light.

The first public lighting was by gas lamps. These required a lamplighter to visit each lamp at twilight, rest his ladder on the crossbars and light the lamp. He would return at dawn to extinguish the flame. This was a very labour intensive method of providing light. Today gas lamp standards can be seen in various locations in the county, including the ones at Carrickbrennan Road (main picture) and Mounttown Roundabout (below left). Old lanterns now are frequently seen with flowers attached to the crossbar!

Electricity was much more efficient. Early electric lighting in the 1800s was created by arc lights. There are many arc light poles still to be seen like the one in Heronsford Lane (above left). They emitted a very harsh light not suitable for ordinary streets and they were superceded by incandescent bulbs. Today HPS (High Pressure Sodium) lamps provide the best illumination for the least consumption of electricity.

...HOW MUCH STREET LIGHTING HAS CHANGED
OVER THE YEARS

?

Previously published by the Heritage Office of Dún Laoghaire-Rathdown County Council.

In Honour & Memory

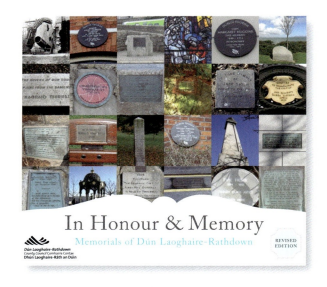

In Honour & Memory

Memorials of Dún Laoghaire-Rathdown

Dún Laoghaire-Rathdown
County Council Comhairle Contae
Dhún Laoghaire-Ráth an Dúin

REVISED EDITION

It looks at the public memorials of Dún Laoghaire-Rathdown. They are important physical reminders of what are often intangible aspects of our identity. The range is bewilderingly eclectic! Available in Local Book shops and Council offices in Dún Laoghaire, or directly from the Heritage Office. Tel. 01-205-4868 email: tcarey@dlrcoco.ie or write to Heritage Officer, County Hall, Dún Laoghaire, County Dublin. Price €10.